NOEL COWARD

LITERATURE AND LIFE: BRITISH WRITERS

Selected list of titles:

Complete list of titles in the series available from publisher on request. Some titles are also in paperback.

NOEL COWARD

Robert F. Kiernan

Ungar • New York

1986
The Ungar Publishing Company
370 Lexington Avenue, New York, N.Y. 10017

Copyright © 1986 by The Ungar Publishing Company

Printed in the United States of America

Library of Congress Cataloging-in-Publication Data

Kiernan, Robert F.
  Noel Coward.

  (Literature and life series)
  Bibliography: p.
  Includes index.
  1. Coward, Noel, 1899–1973 – Criticism and
interpretation.   I. Title.   II. Series.
PR6005.085Z64   1986   822'.912   86-16103
ISBN 0-8044-2456-X

Grateful acknowledgment is made to The Overlook Press for
permission to quote from *The Lyrics of Noel Coward*; Copyright © 1965 by Noel Coward, Published by The Overlook
Press, Lewis Hollow Road, Woodstock, New York 12498; Price:
$25.00.

For Ernie and Ann Speranza

di tutto cuore

Contents

Acknowledgments

The reader will notice in these pages a bare minimum of quotation from Noel Coward's dramatic works. Permission to quote more extensively from the plays was withheld by the Estate of Noel Coward.

Indebtedness in other areas is gratefully acknowledged. For their encouragement and advice, I wish to thank Evander Lomke, my editor at The Ungar Publishing Company, Philip Winsor of The Pennsylvania State University Press, who suggested the project while a senior editor at Ungar, Professor John Nagle, who read an early draft of the manuscript, and Professor Mary Ann O'Donnell, who read portions of an early draft. I am grateful to the staffs of the Manhattan College Library, the New York Public Library, the Theatre Collection at Lincoln Center, the British Library, and the National Portrait Gallery in London for many courtesies — grateful especially to Máire Duchon, who arranged many interlibrary loans, and to Professor Colin Campbell-Hill, who helped me to penetrate recesses of the British Library. Not least of all, I am grateful to Professor Ernest Speranza, who kindly volunteered to proofread the manuscript.

Part of the research for this study was funded by a grant-in-aid from Manhattan College.

Chronology

1928   Writes book, music, and lyrics for *This Year of Grace!* (1928) and appears in US production.

1929   Writes *Bitter Sweet* (1929) and *Private Lives* (1930).

1930   Appears in British production of *Private Lives*. Writes *Post-Mortem* (1968) and begins *Cavalcade* (1931).

1931   Appears in US production of *Private Lives*. *Private Lives* filmed.

1932   Writes book, music, and lyrics for *Words and Music* (1932). Writes *Design for Living* (1933). *The Queen Was in the Parlour* filmed a second time as *Tonight Is Ours*. *Cavalcade* filmed.

1933   Appears in US production of *Design for Living*. Writes *Conversation Piece* (1934). *Design for Living* and *Bitter Sweet* filmed. *Spangled Unicorn* published.

1934   Appears in British production of *Conversation Piece*. Writes *Point Valaine* (1934).

1935   Writes *Tonight at 8:30* (1935) and appears in British production. Appears in film *The Scoundrel*.

1936   Appears in US production of *Tonight at 8:30*.

1937   Writes *Operette* (1938). *Present Indicative* published.

1938   Adapts *Words and Music* for US production as *Set to Music*.

1939   Writes *Present Laughter* (1942) and *This Happy Breed* (1942). *To Step Aside* published.

1940   Tours Australia and writes *Time Remembered* (unproduced).

1941   Tours New Zealand. Writes and directs *Blithe Spirit* (1941). Writes screenplay for *In Which We Serve*. Prosecuted by Finance Defense Department.

1942 Appears in and codirects *In Which We Serve*.
      Appears in British productions of *Blithe Spirit*,
      Present Laughter, and *This Happy Breed*. *We
      Were Dancing* (from *Tonight at 8:30*) filmed.
1943 Appears in British productions of *Present
      Laughter* and *This Happy Breed*.
1944 Tours in South Africa, Far East, and Europe.
      Writes screenplay for *Brief Encounter* (based
      on *Still Life* from *Tonight at 8:30*). *Blithe
      Spirit* filmed. *Middle East Diary* published.
1945 Writes *Sigh No More* (1945) and begins
      Pacific 1860 (1946). Moves into "White
      Cliffs," St. Margaret's Bay, Kent.
1946 Begins *Peace in Our Time* (1947).
1947 Appears in British production of *Present
      Laughter*. Writes *Long Island Sound* (unpro-
      duced).
1948 Appears in French production of *Present
      Laughter*. Writes screenplay for *The Aston-
      ished Heart* (from *Tonight at 8:30*). Builds
      house in Blue Harbor, Jamaica.
1949 Appears in *The Astonished Heart* (1949).
      Writes *Ace of Clubs* (1950) and *Home Coloni-
      al* (produced as *Island Fling* in US in 1951
      and in revised form as *South Sea Bubble* in
      Britain in 1956).
1951 Writes *Relative Values* (1951) and *Quadrille*
      (1952). First cabaret appearance in Britain.
      Star Quality published.
1952 *Meet Me Tonight* (from three plays in *Tonight
      at 8:30*) filmed.
1953 Writes *After the Ball* (1954).
1954 Writes *Nude with Violin* (1956). *Future In-
      definite* published.
1955 Cabaret appearance in Las Vegas. Writes and
      appears in *Together with Music* on US televi-
      sion.

1956   Appears in *Blithe Spirit* and *This Happy
        Breed* on US television. Writes *Volcano* (un-
        produced). Divests himself of British property
        and goes into tax exile.

1957   Appears in US production of *Nude with
        Violin*.

1958   Appears in US productions of *Present Laugh-
        ter* and *Nude with Violin*. Adapts Feydeau
        farce as *Look after Lulu* (1959). Composes
        score for ballet *London Morning* (1959).

1959   Begins *Waiting in the Wings* (1960). Buys
        home in Les Avants, Switzerland.

1960   *Pomp and Circumstance* published.

1961   Completes *Sail Away* (1961).

1962   Writes music and lyrics for *The Girl Who
        Came to Supper* (1963).

1964   Directs US production of *High Spirits* (musical
        adaptation of *Blithe Spirit*) and British pro-
        duction of *Hay Fever*. *Pretty Polly Barlow*
        published.

1965   Writes *Suite in Three Keys* (1966).

1966   Appears on West End for last time in *Suite in
        Three Keys*. Begins stage version of *Star Qual-
        ity* (unproduced).

1967   *Bon Voyage* and *Not Yet the Dodo* published.

1970   Knighted.

1972   *Cowardly Custard* produced in Britain and
        Oh! Coward in US.

1973   Dies March 26 in Jamaica.

MEMORANDUM OF SERVICE NOT SUPPLIED

Book .... Information .... Magazine .... Pamphlet ....

Record .... Map .... Film .... Other ....

List below: Title and Author—Subject or Question

....

....

....

Disposition ....

Patron's name and phone if needed ....

....

Staff member's initials .... Date ....

1

The Legend
and the Life

The Noel Coward legend was born one day in 1924 when the sleek young star of *The Vortex* allowed himself to be photographed abed, wearing a Chinese dressing gown and an expression of ripe degeneracy. Reproduced in newspapers the next morning, that picture became an icon of the man who was to be seen taking drugs on stage each evening at the Royalty Theatre, and for the generation known as The Bright Young Things, Noel Coward came to symbolize the spirit of Mayfair rebellion. He was youth brushed with decadence and glamour; he was gaiety and insouciance personified. Somehow, Coward never lost that reputation. The iconography was unchanged thirty years later when the promoters of his Las Vegas show arranged for publicity photographs in the Nevada desert with Coward impossibly nonchalant in a tuxedo. In looking now at those photographs so many years apart, one remembers a line he delivered in *The Scoundrel*: "That's the proper place for life—in one's buttonhole."

Coward generally professed to stand agog before his legend, but he contributed to its growth in many ways. As a young man he was capable of leading cheers for his own plays from the back of the circle, and for a time he made a pet of a coral snake named Eugénie, who occasioned screams when she peered from his breast pocket during cocktail parties. He loved scenes — the more histrionic the better — and he would affect suicidal despair over mislaid cufflinks, fountain pens that soiled his fingers, and leading ladies who cared more for their coiffures than for their craft. Left almost penniless by the expense, he traveled to New York in 1921 via the luxury liner *Aquitania*, the better to establish a reputation for high style. Interviewed by Edward R. Murrow on American television, he was asked if he did anything to relax after a long day's work. "Certainly," he quipped, "but I have no intention of discussing it before several million people." Whimsically, he encouraged his friends and associates to address him as "Master."

Coward's wit was central to his legend. Impatient with Claudette Colbert at a rehearsal for *Blithe Spirit*, he countered her insistence that she had known her lines backward the night before with the acid comment, "And that's just the way you're saying them this morning." The actor Keir Dullea was once unnerved when Coward crept up behind him and whispered in his ear, "Keir Dullea, Gone Tomorrow!" The actor David Niven records an occasion on which one of Coward's many godchildren exclaimed, "Uncle Noel! Look at those two little doggies! What *are* they doing?" Godfather Coward took notice immediately. "The little doggie in front has just gone blind," he explained with avuncular solicitude, "and his friend is pushing him all the way to St. Dunstans."[1] The young Laurence Olivier was cured of a tendency to giggle his way through performances by Coward's invention of a canine named Roger, whom he imagined on stage whenever he and Olivier had a scene together. Roger was naughtily obsessed with Olivier's privates, and under the cloak of invisibility he performed unspeakable acts of sexual aggression. "Roger, not in front of the vicar!" Coward might whisper for Olivier's ears — or, in extremis, a deeply shocked "*Roger!*"[2]

Much of Coward's personal charm sprang from the disparaging tone he adopted toward his legend. He found it amusing that he preferred a postprandial Ovaltine and lots of sleep to all-night carousing, and that he failed on occasion to cut an elegant figure:

The other morning I was caught [by a busload of tourists], practically naked and carrying a frying pan in one hand and a slop-pail in the other. I paused graciously while they took their bloody snapshots, and then pressed on with my tasks and occupations. Noel Coward is *so* sophisticated.[3]

Indeed, the Coward who stood behind the colorful legend was disciplined and self-aware, less The Playboy of the West End than a thoroughly professional Man of the Theater. Alexander Woollcott labeled him "Destiny's Tot," but it was his good fortune, Coward protested, "to have a bright, acquisitive, but not, *not* an intellectual mind, and to have been impelled by circumstances to get out and earn my living."[4] The life eclipsed by his legend was a chronicle of just such humble forces.

Although he was born on December 16, 1899, and liked to think himself a child of the new century, Coward was indubitably the child of his mother, Violet Veitch Coward. Addicted to the theater of Henry Irving and Ellen Terry, she had all the instincts of a stage parent, but she was too unsophisticated in the ways of theatrical employment and too self-consciously genteel to merit the reputation of that breed. Indeed, it seems that she aspired at first only to share her enjoyment of the theater with her favorite son. She took Coward from the age of five to the Christmas pantomimes and from the age of seven to the West End music halls, where he saw Gertie Millar in *The Quaker Girl*, Lily Elsie in *The Merry Widow*, and such veteran performers of the Edwardian theater as Nellie Wallace, George Robey, and Maidie Scott. His formal education was spasmodic, taking second place to skills that could be shown off in the parlor. At a time when Mrs. Coward could little afford the expense, he was enrolled in a dancing academy in Hanover Square. Had he not failed the entrance audition, he would apparently have been enrolled in The Chapel Royal School for choirboys.

His mother's dominant role in young Noel's life had the effect of minimizing other family members in his awareness. His father was a sometime piano tuner who must have lent something to Coward's musical interest, but Arthur Sabin Coward lapsed into insolvency when his sons were young and lapsed thereafter into the shadows of his wife's boarding house. A younger brother named Eric lived less completely in the shadows, but he never engaged Coward's feelings until sickness and death claimed him in 1933. That Mrs. Coward and Noel were deeply self-centered had much to do with this unbalanced sense of family, but the crowdedness of Coward's professional life from the age of fourteen also decreed the imbalance, at least in part. Because she shared his love for the theater and spoke up more assertively than father or brother for a share of his concern, Mrs. Coward received what obeisance Coward had in him to give. He supported her in comfort until her death in 1954, extended her his arm at opening-night performances, and memorialized her taste for gratuitous quarrels in many of his plays.

Coward's first professional appearance was at the age of eleven in *The Goldfish*, a fairy play produced by Lila Field's Children's Theatre. When informed by the producer that her son's fee would be a guinea and a half a week, Mrs. Coward was so inexperienced she thought she was to be charged the fee. Young Noel was quicker than she to learn the professional ropes, and he was shortly visiting the agencies and negotiating fees on his own. He snared a two-month run in *The Great Name*, in which Charles Hawtrey starred, and a subsequent engagement in Hawtrey's production of the children's classic *Where the Rainbow Ends*. Two other youngsters destined for fame, Hermione Gingold and Brian Aherne, also appeared in that production.

By the age of twelve, Coward fancied himself a professional actor, and his schooling thereafter was even more irregular than before. Other engagements followed upon *Where the Rainbow Ends*: the role of a toadstool in the ballet *An Autumn Idyll*; a sketch with Hawtrey called "A Little Fowl Play" in a variety bill at the Coliseum; a double part in a Basil Dean production of Hauptmann's *Hannele*, in which fifteen-year-old Gertrude Lawrence also appeared; the role of Slightly in a production of *Peter Pan*, then in its eleventh year at the Duke of York's Theatre. Coward impressed Hawtrey and others with whom he worked as an energetic and quick young man. It was clear to everyone that he was determined to make his way in the theater. The diaeresis with which he adorned the *e* of his forename at the age of fourteen was public promise that the name would one day be famous.

World War I touched Coward very little. England declared war on Germany on August 4, 1914, and the brooding, mustached face of Lord Kitchener was soon on posters everywhere, pointing an accusing finger over a caption that said, "Your King and Country Need You Now." Coward had no sense that the Minister of War was pointing at him. Too young to enlist for the first three and a half years of the war, he was not called before the Army Medical Board until January 1918, and not found physically fit until a second medical examination several months later. Like some others of his generation, he was bored by the universal smear of khaki and had little impulse to become part of the war effort. "Four futile years . . . robbed even bravery of its glamour," he wrote in his autobiography, "and the far greater gallantry of courage in the face of anti-climax was too remote for dejected civilians to grasp. It was certainly too abstract an ideal to inspire a self-centered young actor."[5]

Thus, the self-centered young actor pursued his career unswervingly. In December 1915 he returned to *Where the Rainbow Ends* to play the role of the Slacker (too grown, now, for his former role of the page boy), and in the spring he joined a touring production of *Charley's Aunt*. A small part in a short-lived musical called *The Light Blues* followed in the summer of 1916, and Christmas of that year found him once again in a children's play, *The Happy Family*, in which he played a Sandhurst cadet. A momentary appearance pushing a wheelbarrow in D. W. Griffith's *Hearts of the World* marked his inauspicious film debut.

The opportunity that every actor awaits proved elusive until the summer of 1917, when the American impresario Gilbert Miller saw Coward's performance during a three-week run of *Wild Heather* in Manchester and engaged him to play the juvenile lead in a West End production of *The Saving Grace*. "He had come down *specially* to see me," Coward could boast in a letter to his mother, for Charles Hawtrey, who was also to appear in the Haddon Chambers comedy, had advised Miller to engage the young man who had dogged his footsteps for years. He had apparently forgiven Coward the pestiferous questioning that once caused him to miss an entrance.

Hawtrey's patronage helped to write Coward's theatrical future, but it was Gilbert Miller who gave direction to Coward's sense of himself as a writer. Having already experimented with the writing of poems and lyrics, Coward was sufficiently flattered by the impresario's show of interest to attempt scriptwriting, and by the end of 1918 he had shown the great man three plays, one of them *The Rat Trap*. Not greatly impressed, Miller shared with Coward his belief that a play's dialogue had to be secondary to its construction. His belief became Coward's creed — a crucial discipline upon his besetting love for the quip. "As long as I continue to write plays to be acted in theatres," he wrote years later, "I shall strain every fibre to see that they are clear, well constructed and strong enough in content, either serious or funny, to keep an average paying audience interested from 8:30 till 11:15. Here endeth the first and last and, for me, only lesson."[6]

In fact, however, Miller's was not the only lesson. Coward was an eager student at this time of anyone willing to teach him, and he attached himself parasitically to those he admired. The same Manchester run during which Miller offered him advice saw Ivy St. Helier teaching him piano "authority" — the commanding chords with which he was to claim audiences' attention for the rest of his life. A year later, the ingenue Mary Robson advanced his musical education by introducing him to French opera and operetta. In 1921 the example of Katherine Cornell and Tallulah Bankhead in *Nice People* taught him to play for speed in the first act of a comedy and for laughter in the third.

When finally called up for war service, Coward found army life intolerable. "Truly the war had made masochists of us all,"[7] Vera Brittain opined, but she was not thinking of Coward. "The need of my King and Country seemed unimportant compared with the vital necessity of forging ahead with my own career," he wrote in *Present Indicative*. "It was a matter of pressing urgency to me that I should become rich and successful as soon as possible."[8] His B2 medical classification suggested a way out of the army. Self-induced headaches and high temperatures gradually became psychosomatic and uncontrollable; months of hospitalization ensued; and nine months after his induction, Coward received a medical discharge from the Artists' Rifles. In December 1918 he was appearing again in the West End in a play called *Scandals*.

In the immediate postwar years, Coward developed a reputation more as a promising new playwright than

as an actor. He turned to writing during this period
largely to relieve the tedium of playing the same role
night after night. Such early plays as *The Rat Trap*
(1926),[9] *Sirocco* (1927), and *The Queen Was in the Parlour* (1926) are well forgotten, but *I'll Leave It to You*
(1920) has the distinction of having achieved a West End
run when Coward was legally too young to sign the
necesary contracts. *The Young Idea* (1922) earned him
not only good reviews but a kindly letter of advice from
George Bernard Shaw, to whose *You Never Can Tell*
Coward's play was deeply indebted.[10] His reputation
was increasingly based on his wit, and the charmingly
vacuous prattle at which he excelled was thought quintessentially à la mode. "She's got no go in her that girl,"
says Eustace in *The Young Idea*. "She borrowed the top
of my Thermos and never returned it. Shallow, very
shallow." Such lines became the hallmark of a Coward
comedy. Songs and sketches also proliferated from Coward's free moments during these years. His contributions
to the André Charlot revue *London Calling!* (1923) were
generally admired, particularly a burlesque of the Sitwells entitled "The Swiss Family Whittlebot."

In writing and directing *The Vortex* (1924), Coward was conscious mainly of creating "a whacking good
part" for himself in the character of the drug addict Nicky
Lancaster. He created for himself not only a great part
but an international reputation. Like John Osborne's
Look Back in Anger thirty years later, the play was an
overnight sensation in that it seemed to speak unflinch-
ingy for the contemporary generation and to herald a
new zeitgeist. An unexpected drift in the play from comedy to near-tragedy was thought particularly nasty —
paricularly *true* — and parents en masse tried to shield
young adults from the play's harsh disclosures by forbid-
ding them to attend. "Poor soulless, rotten 1924," grieved
a drama critic on the *Daily Graphic*. "There's some consolation in having grown up before the war. Some critics

have complained that Nicky and Bunty are not true to life. I seem to meet them everywhere."[11]

Not entirely to his pleasure, Coward emerged from the success of *The Vortex* a spokesman for those who seemed to greet the dissolution of all values with an immoderate quest for sensation. The first fruits of this spokesmanship were pleasant, with photographs in the popular press and stages made available for his next works. But a lifetime of having to answer for a hedonistic philosophy that he neither espoused nor lived by was a more lasting fruit that Coward found bittersweet.

Even before he found fame as the author of *The Vortex*, Coward had found entrance to the homes of the rich and famous. He frankly liked celebrities, and in 1922 he could number among his acquaintances such titans as Arnold Bennett, John Galsworthy, Somerset Maugham, Compton MacKenzie, Hugh Walpole, H. G. Wells, and Rebecca West. His close friends already included Gertrude Lawrence, Alfred Lunt and Lynn Fontanne, the novelist Joyce Carey, and the designer Edward Molyneux. As an accomplished conversationalist and a willing entertainer at the piano, he paid his social dues, and with the prestige of *The Vortex* to complement his natural amiableness, he was taken up by such hostesses as Lady Colefax and Elsa Maxwell. His tendency to cultivate the rich and famous was noted over the years, but forgiven. Sir Henry Channon describes him tellingly in his diaries as "an arch-flatterer," "insinuating, pathetic and nice."[12] Part of his niceness was the instinctive sympathy he extended to those in emotional pain. Vivien Leigh always kept with her a warm and moving letter he wrote her during one of her breakdowns.

Surprisingly, Coward never lost his head to the society he adored, even in the intoxication of these early years. His self-imposed disciplines of work and writing remained firm, and with an instinctive sense of self-preservation he began to gather about him the "family"

of employees and coworkers that was to anchor him in
the workaday world. The charter members of his so-
called family were Lorn Loraine, who served as his secretary-manager until her death in 1967; Gladys Calthrop,
who handled set and costume design for most of Coward's plays until the early 1950s; and John Chapman
Wilson, who served for many years as Coward's financial
advisor, later as his American agent. Cole Lesley and
Graham Payn were later to join the family in more intimate roles, Lesley as Coward's factotum, and Payn in
an amorphous role as Lesley's assistant.[13]

Suddenly in demand after his success with *The Vortex*, Coward stepped almost immediately into an association with the great showman C. B. Cochran, whose revues at the London Pavilion were becoming a national
institution, much as Florenz Ziegfeld's revues had already become in America. The revue *On with the Dance*
(1925), for which Coward wrote the book, lyrics, and
most of the music, was the first production of their nine-
year association and an entire success. Alice Delysia's
singing of "Poor Little Rich Girl" is alleged to have started
all London humming. *Fallen Angels*, which Coward
had written in 1923, was put into production during the
concurrent runs of *The Vortex* and *On with the Dance*
and slipped into the West End for a four-month run. A
drawing-room comedy about two women who await the
visit of a lover they shared before their marriages, it offered titillations that infuriated the moralistic press. So
violent was the newspaper harangue ("Disgusting!" "Ob-
scene!" "Those Soused Sluts!"), that Coward found it
amusing to forswear his reputation as a decadent. "The
realization that I am hopelessly depraved, vicious, and
decadent has for two days ruined my morning beaker of
opium," he reassured readers of the *Sunday Chronicle*.
"I find I no longer enjoy my four o'clock cocaine tablets,
and I have flung my hypodermic needle into the Thames

with the firm resolution of turning over a new leaf and for the future I intend to write only the healthiest of healthy plays, dealing exclusively with birth, marriage, and death in the open air."[14]

In the two years following the production of *Fallen Angels*, Coward wrote three more comedies, *This Was a Man* (1926), *The Marquise* (1927), and *Home Chat* (1927), but only *The Marquise* enjoyed even modest success. When the early plays *The Rat Trap* (1926) and *Sirocco* (1927) failed dismally in post-*Vortex* production, Coward's fans began to fear that the wunderkind was only a nine-days' wonder. In fact, however, Coward was on the verge of his brightest, most golden period as a dramatist. Later in his life he would acknowledge that this string of failures in the wake of his success had been painfully salutary, a bracingly cold bath, as it were, in the waters of fickle fame.

During the period 1928 to 1934, each year saw the production of a new Coward play or revue: *This Year of Grace!* in 1928, *Bitter Sweet* in 1929, *Private Lives* in 1930, *Cavalcade* in 1931, *Words and Music* in 1932, *Design for Living* in 1933, *Conversation Piece* in 1934. All but *Design for Living* were under the Cochran banner, and all were extravagantly acclaimed. So numerous and so impassioned were Coward's fans during this period, that when he appeared with Alfred Lunt and Lynn Fontanne in the American production of *Design for Living*, special police had to be called out to control the street crowds for the last two months of the run. Coward was even compelled to employ a bodyguard for the first and only time in his life.

Fans announced themselves in high places as well as low. Arnold Bennett was allegedly the first to murmur "The Congreve of Our Day," but the phrase was soon a commonplace among the literati. Impressed, no doubt, that Coward had matched his record of four plays running concurrently in the West End, Somerset Maugham treated the young playwright to a deference as extravagant as that accorded him in the streets of New York:

For us English dramatists the young generation has assumed the brisk but determined form of Mr. Noël Coward. He knocked at the door with impatient knuckles, and then he rattled the handle, and then he burst in. After a moment's stupor the older playwrights welcomed him affably enough and retired with what dignity they could muster to the shelf which with a spritely gesture he indicated to them as their proper place . . . and since there is no one now writing who has more obviously a gift for the theatre than Mr. Noël Coward, nor more influence with young writers, it is probably his inclination and practice that will be responsible for the manner in which plays will be written during the next twenty years.[15]

Coward had not earned such encomiums without paying a price. Two years of a frenetic pace and over-stretched nerves came to a head in the fall of 1926 when he played a whole performance of Margaret Kennedy's *The Constant Nymph* with tears of exhaustion running down his cheeks. A week in bed and a voyage to New York, where he was to start rehearsals for *This Was a Man*, failed to restore his nerves. Sleep — always his consolation — began to elude him, and he seems to have feared for his sanity. By Christmas he was running a fever of 103 degrees without any obvious physical cause, just as he had earlier run such a fever in the army. Recuperating in Hawaii, he took himself to task for burning the candle at both ends. "From now onwards," he wrote in his autobiography, "there was going to be very little energy wasted, and very little vitality spilled unnecessarily." Although a gregarious man, his isolation on a ranch in Hawaii led him to conclude that a press of people threatened his equilibrium. "People, I decided, were the danger. People were greedy and predatory, and if you gave them the chance, they would steal unscrupulously the heart and soul out of you without really wanting to or even meaning to."[16]

There can be little question that Coward was prone to psychosomatic illness whenever the circumstances of life threatened to unbalance him. If he was temperamentally self-centered, this aspect of his personality was the blind side of an engagement in his projects so total that it tended to consume him utterly. Incapacitating illnesses were his balance beam, a subconscious refusal to let himself slip into misanthropy. After his near breakdown in 1926, he moderated his life and his human relationships more carefully. He accepted no theatrical engagements for the whole of 1927, and he purchased a country home in Kent known as Goldenhurst Farm, to which he retreated regularly to bask in the sun that was almost as restorative a pleasure for him as sleep. It is arguable that without the nervous crisis of 1927 and the self-disciplines that it compelled, Coward could not have sustained the creative output of 1928–1934.

Coward's influence on the British theater did not prove as seminal as Somerset Maugham predicted, but it was by no means negligible. His plays of the late twenties opened the theater to a more sophisticated level of comedic insight than London was previously able to enjoy, and his crisp dialogue was the death blow to Edwardian declamation—a climax to Shaw's campaign to free the British theater from the nineteenth century. The impress of Coward's personal style upon his characters was so definitive that Kenneth Tynan wrote in 1953, "Even the youngest of us will know in fifty years time what we mean by 'a very Noël Coward sort of person.'"[17]

Indeed, Coward's sense of personal style shaped not only the theatrical stage but the stage of life. His exaggeratedly clipped speech and his breezily insouciant manner were imitated both onstage and off. In emulation of his stage dialogue, it became fashionable to apply the authority of experience to the most frivolous subjects and to interject the patois of jazz into serious discussion as readily as into cocktail chatter. Coward's manner of calling the most solemn endeavors "lots of fun" and of peppering every sentence with the adjective "terribly" became endemic in fashionable speech, and all sorts of men transformed themselves into Noel Coward look-alikes, slick and satiny. The world of fashion also took cues from Coward. His wearing of crewneck pullovers was much imitated after his success in *The Vortex*, and his sumptuous dressing gowns worn over trousers, shirt, and tie became acceptable attire in drawing rooms. His bow ties, his brown dinner-jacket suits, and the white silk scarves he affected with navy blue casual clothes had unmeasurable influence among the sartorially conscious.

The premiere of *Cavalcade* in 1931 gave a deeper and more serious orientation to Coward's influence. An opening-night audience worried by Britain's imminent abandonment of the gold standard saw Coward's thirty-year panorama of English life as a triumphant vindication of the English spirit, and they applauded its author lustily. Coward did not understand himself to have written a patriotic play, but seizing upon the mood of the moment, he gave an impromptu speech which concluded, "In spite of the troublous times we live in, it is still pretty exciting to be English." For an important segment of the British people, he became at that moment a spokesman for homeland and hearth. His identification with the Bright Young Things (aging now into the Smart Set) assumed the status of a camp affectation and seemed no longer the threat to national morals that it had been. Lord Beaverbrook's newspapers accused him of jingoism, but King George V and Queen Mary attended a performance of *Cavalcade* in celebration of a sweeping National Government election victory, and Coward was thereafter a favorite of the Royal Family.

Although amused at first by this recasting of his public image, Coward grew steadily into the role of patriot and made it his own. *Present Laughter*, his most autobiographically revealing play, suggests the transformation. Written in 1939, it is the story of Garry Essendine, a writer who has given himself up so entirely to role playing that he represses the man he really is. That Coward was rethinking his own persona is suggested not only by the theme of *Present Laughter* but also by his immediately subsequent writing of *This Happy Breed* (1942), a play which returns to *Cavalcade*'s theme of English staunchness as if to reaffirm its patriotic stance. No longer the self-centered young man who had avoided service in World War I, the author of *Cavalcade* was preparing a role for himself in the coming war.

The War Office, however, found little enthusiasm for Coward's contribution, and most of his attempts to help the war effort turned to gall in his mouth. Implementing a wit's-end suggestion from Minister of Information Duff Cooper that he embark on a goodwill tour of America, he found his mission ridiculed by the Beaverbrook press and his activities questioned in the House of Commons. The publication of his *Middle East Diary* (1944), which he hoped would be inspirational, had the unfortunate effect of making his troop concerts in North Africa seem a holiday de luxe at government expense. The cruelest blow was a strange prosecution by the Finance Defense Department when he failed to declare the financial holdings in America that had supported him on his government assignment. He could point with some pride to a series of patriotic songs that contributed something to Britain's morale, most notably "London Pride," but a popular misunderstanding of his satire in the song "Don't Let's Be Beastly to the Germans" seemed to sour even this war work. He could point with considerable pride, however, to the film *In Which We Serve* (1942), which he wrote, starred in, and codirected. A tribute to his friend Lord Mountbatten and the crew of the H.M.S. *Kelly*, it was a major work of British naval propaganda and earned the unqualified praise of both Churchill and King George VI. Germany was sufficiently impressed by Coward's war work to include his name on the famous Black List of those who were to be executed when Germany won the war. When the Black List was published, Rebecca West sent The Master a telegram:

MY DEAR THE PEOPLE WE SHOULD HAVE BEEN SEEN DEAD WITH![18]

After the war, Coward's reputation as a playwright went into decline, perhaps inevitably. As Lady Markby warns in Wilde's *An Ideal Husband*, "Nothing is so dangerous as being too modern. One is apt to grow old-fashioned quite suddenly." Coward appealed largely to the camp taste, and the postwar mood of the theater was abruptly conservative, espousing the verse plays of Christopher Fry, the light comedies and psychological melodramas of Terence Rattigan, and such blockbuster American musicals as *Annie Get Your Gun*, *Oklahoma*, and *Carousel*. The postwar mood was also republican, and having contributed to the decline of British nobility by making his dukes and duchesses so witty that the real ones seemed moribund, Coward found his stage aristocrats out of fashion. Lord Beaverbrook's animosity for the Coward cult, expressed for many years through his newspapers, also diminished Coward's reputation.

Anti-Coward invective even became something of a sport after the war. The actor George Devine compared Coward sourly and too memorably to "a well-paid chorus girl."[19] Indulging a mood of unbridled snideness, the Irish dramatist Sean O'Casey launched a series of essays attacking Coward and announced, "Noel Coward hasn't yet put even his nose into the front rank of second-class dramatists, let alone into the front rank of first-class dramatists."[20]

Coward's postwar decline has been exaggerated,

however, both by Coward himself and by those who
have commented on his career. While he was not in those
years the West End idol that he had been, his personal
mystique survived the demise of the Smart Set, and he
played only to full and enthusiastic houses whenever he
appeared in one of his own works. A certain number of
his postwar plays were commercial failures — the revue
Pacific 1860 (1946), *Peace in Our Time* (1947) — but the
majority of his postwar offerings had satisfactory West
End runs. They failed to satisfy The Master, one suspects,
only in comparison with *Blithe Spirit* (1941), whose run
of four and a half years had been one of the longest in
London theater history. The typical Coward play ran for
slightly less than a year, both before the war and after.
Ace of Clubs (1950), which Coward thought a flop, fell
short of *The Vortex* by only twenty-three performances.
The revue *South Sea Bubble* (1956) surpassed the run of
On with the Dance; *Relative Values* (1951) ran longer
than *Cavalcade*; and *Quadrille* (1952) ran for a year and
four months despite reviews Coward thought "patroniz-
ing and contemptuous."[21] The glitter may have worn
off his reputation, but the commercial viability of Coward's work was little changed.

Among the several factors which made Coward
question his postwar success was a greater need for money. The royalties that had seemed lavish in 1924 when
they allowed the author of *The Vortex* to purchase silk
pajamas and redecorate his bedroom in scarlet were
barely adequate in 1954 to finance his extensive traveling, to support his personal and professional staffs, and
to maintain Goldenhurst Farm, his flat in Belgravia, and
his lavish vacation retreat in Jamaica. As he had no cap-
ital funds and lived solely on royalties and fees, Inland
Revenue taxes between twenty-five thousand pounds
and fifty thousand pounds each year threatened him
with insolvency. In 1956 he looked Father Time in the
face and saw his financial position as acute. His decision

was to give up Goldenhurst Farm and the Belgravia flat and to escape the Chancellor of the Exchequer by living abroad. A familiar tax ploy today, this maneuver was thought dastardly in 1956 — especially to be deplored in the creator of *Cavalcade* and *In Which We Serve*. As a result, Coward had to suffer the outrage of both press and friends in what must have seemed to him a reprise of the furor over his World War II activities. The plaguy bill was only slightly meliorated by the success of *South Sea Bubble, Nude with Violin* (1956), and a series of appearances on American television. In his last diary entry for 1956 he confessed to "a certain change of heart regarding my own country," "a core of sadness," "a little private menopause as well."[22]

Occasional work for the film industry helped Coward to survive his several financial crises. Always penny-wise, he seldom rejected the ancillary projects that are proposed to actors and writers. In 1921, the editor of *Metropolitan* offered him five hundred dollars to turn *I'll Leave It to You* into a short story, and Coward remarked that for such a princely sum he would consider turning *War and Peace* into a music-hall sketch. Fourteen of his plays were adapted for the screen within his lifetime, and some of those films achieved classic status, notably Sidney Franklin's *Private Lives* (1931), Ernst Lubitsch's *Design for Living* (1933), and Frank Lloyd's unfaithful but stylish *Cavalcade* (1932). Other adaptations sank into obscurity with Coward's blessing. A 1940 American remake of the 1933 British film version of *Bitter Sweet* seemed to him "like watching an affair between a mad rocking-horse and a rawhide suitcase."[23] "It really is frightening," he wrote, "that the minds of Hollywood could cheerfully perpetrate such a nauseating hotchpotch of vulgarity, false values, seedy dialogue, stale sentiment, vile performances and abominable direction."[24]

In the wake of *Bitter Sweet's* leathery ravage, Coward went through a period of assuming production and scriptwriting chores himself, first in his wartime opus *In Which We Serve*, subsequently in the films *This Happy Breed* (1944), *Brief Encounter* (1945), *Blithe Spirit* (1945), and *The Astonished Heart* (1949). He also worked occasionally as a film actor. His starring performance in *The Scoundrel* (1935) was a minor triumph of his career, and he enjoyed a profitable employment as a character actor in the films *Around the World in Eighty Days* (1956), *Our Man in Havana* (1959), *Surprise Package* (1960), *Paris When It Sizzles* (1963), *Bunny Lake Is Missing* (1965), *Boom!* (1968), and *The Italian Job* (1969).

The combination of Coward's long quest for financial security and his professional intrepidity spurred still another career as he approached old age—that of a cabaret performer. In June 1951 he gave a series of intimate concerts for the benefit of the Actors' Orphanage, and the success of those concerts inspired him to work up an act for the Café de Paris, a fashionable London nightclub. His voice was hardly a good one ("the cooing of a baritone dove," Kenneth Tynan once called it[25]), but he had an actor's tricks of phrasing and inflection and a stage presence that was magisterial. His instant, acclaimed success was due to panache and performance rather than sonority. He went on to further engagements at the Café de Paris and, in 1955, to a justly famous triumph in Las Vegas.

Coward made a conscious decision when preparing these cabaret performances to render his songs straightforwardly. "Nobody seems capable of leaving well enough alone and allowing the words to take care of themselves," he complained in his diary. "Neither my lyrics nor my dialogue require decoration; all they do require are clarity, diction and intention and a minimum of gesture and business."[26] Yet both his cabaret performances and his acting were unquestionably camp, depending for their appeal on a complex of controlled mannerisms and obvious exaggerations. Coward never quite understood, it seems, how deeply artificial his manner was. His affectation of an upper-class accent resulted actually in a manner of speech no man ever spoke, almost a parody of upper-class British speech. The raised eyebrow that he fancied the height of elegance was actually a gesture delicately epicene. Because such camp manners were perfectly adapted to the songs he tended to feature— songs like "Mad Dogs and Englishmen" and "I've Been to a Marvelous Party"—his cabaret performances succeeded brilliantly.

This inability on Coward's part to acknowledge his camping suggests a failure to come to terms with the homosexuality his camping expressed. It is no secret that he was homosexual, nor that he hated the self-exposure and emotional loss of control he experienced the four or five times he fell seriously in love. But he also hated female impersonators, thought Oscar Wilde "one of the silliest, most conceited and unattractive characters that ever existed,"[27] and found the homosexual community on New York's Fire Island "sick-sick-sick."[28] Such attitudes suggest an antihomosexual streak within his homosexuality—a self-contempt, ultimately, that must have censored his awareness of how he flirted with sexual disclosure in his mannerisms.

Coward's success as a cabaret performer tended to eclipse his reputation as a playwright and even to create an impression he had misplayed his talent over the years. *Waiting in the Wings* (1960) is his best postwar play and might have been a commercial success but for the insistence of drama critics that he was theatrically passé. Coward described the reviews as a "ghastly cold douche" and confessed to feeling "frankly miserable."[29] He vented his pique by writing a series of articles critical of the contemporary theater,[30] but the articles were curmudgeonly and seemed further evidence that he was dramatically out of date. The New York run of *Sail Away* (1961), the last play for which he bore the combined responsibility of author, composer, lyricist, and director, was hardly more encouraging than the London run of *Waiting in the Wings*. In his Jamaican hideaway he took stock and wondered if he had lost touch with the times: "Have I really, or at least nearly, reached the crucial moment when I should retire from the fray and spend my remaining years sorting out my memories and sentimentalizing the past at the expense of the present?"[31]

Such questioning was doomed by Coward's habitual optimism, and two years later his diary records a very different mood. "The Noël Coward renaissance," he noted coolly, "is in full swing."[32] A number of factors account for the change in reputation to which he alluded, most notably the successful revival of *Private Lives* in 1963 and of *Hay Fever* in 1964. Of more subtle importance was a gathering realization that Coward's writing could be understood as stylishly period rather than as crudely old-fashioned. Almost overnight, it seemed, he was a grand old man of the theater — sui generis — "The Master." J. B. Priestley could ask Coward in 1964, "What is all this nonsense about you being called the Master?"[33] precisely because the appellation was no longer a joke.

Much to Coward's gratification, his renaissance brought critical nosegays. A musical adaptation of *Blithe Spirit* under the title *High Spirits* (1964) won plaudits for his direction and original authorship, and the success of *Suite in Three Keys* (1966) was all he could have desired, with fine press notices and crowds of fans clamoring nightly for the autographs he never denied them. A knighthood deferred since 1943 was announced in the New Year's List for 1970, giving a royal imprimatur to his rehabilitation in the theater, and BBC-TV marked the occasion of his knighthood with a week-long festival of Coward films and a testimonial dinner at the Savoy. The American Theatre Wing honored him with a special

Tony award for Distinguished Achievement in the Theatre, and hit revues on both sides of the Atlantic anthologized scenes and songs from his plays — *Cowardly Custard* (1972) in London, *Oh! Coward* (1972) in New York. In old age he became, as he often joked, "a National Treasure."

Much as he enjoyed this belatedly generous acclaim, it remained irksome to Coward that his personal mystique inveighed against his reputation as a writer. "I think on the whole I am a better writer than I am given credit for being," he had complained years before in his diary. "It is fairly natural that my writing should be casually appreciated because my personality, performances, music and legend get in the way. Some day, I suspect, when Jesus has definitely got me for a sunbeam, my works may be adequately assessed."[34] He was thinking not only of playscripts he wrote under the hope of immediate production, but of nondramatic works he had written in his passion to make good use of every moment. Such writing did not always summon his powers fully. The satires of *A Withered Nosegay* (1922), *Chelsea Buns* (1924), and *Spangled Unicorn* (1933) are amusing but youthfully slapdash, and the autobiographical volumes *Present Indicative* (1937) and *Future Indefinite* (1954) are heavy with undigested fact and observation, not at all the romps one might expect. Later writings are more carefully wrought than these, inasmuch as they had to fulfill Coward's need for a sense of industry as his vacations in the sun became more obviously self-indulgent. He turned his hand to the novel in *Pomp and Circumstance* (1960), to short stories in the collections *Pretty Polly Barlow* (1964) and *Bon Voyage* (1967), and to an anthology of his verse in *Not Yet the Dodo* (1967).

In the afterglow of his renaissance, Coward's sense of professional urgency began to fade. Arteriosclerosis exacted a toll from the phenomenal memory that had allowed him to sing "Mad Dogs and Englishmen" at tri-

ple speed, and to his great embarrassment he found himself forgetting his lines during the run of *Suite in Three
Keys* and the filming of *Boom!* and *The Italian Job*. The
deaths of his friends Winifred Ashton (Clemence Dane)
in 1965 and of Vivien Leigh and Lorn Loraine in 1967
shook him badly. Walking became a slow, painful process, and half in jest, half seriously, he began to affect
the manner of one frail and aged. The last volume of his
autobiography was abandoned incomplete, and he dis-
continued keeping his diary at the end of 1969. In the
certainty that his reputation was secure, he allowed himself to relax, to spend long afternoons in his studio paint-
ing brightly colored canvases in the company of Cole
Lesley and Graham Payn; to enjoy his friends, his win-
ters at Blue Harbor, Jamaica, and his summers at Les
Avants, Switzerland; to take in 1968 one last round-the-
world journey. Suspicious that death was approaching,
he planned his last words — a Voltairean "Les flammes
déjà?" — and worried he would die screaming "Bugger
off!" at some officious nurse. He died without nurses,
easily, after an apparent heart attack on the morning of
March 26, 1973, at his home in Jamaica.

Of all the words of eulogy that poured out across
the world in succeeding weeks, none were so apt as those
of Sir John Betjeman. At a memorial service in the church
of St. Martin-in-the-Fields, he likened that "beautiful,
great eighteenth-century theatre of a church" to Coward's
aristocratic spirit. "Cheerful, wide, welcoming English
baroque," he mused, "it is precise, elegant, and well-
ordered. Like Noël."[35]

2

The Comedies of Manners

Although he professed to despise the comedy of manners,[1] Coward wrote some of the twentieth century's best examples of the genre, and almost all his plays contain its elements. It was inevitably so, for the repartee that enlivens the comedy of manners was Coward's especial talent both onstage and off, and the polished and sophisticated society that the comedy of manners satirizes was his chosen milieu. It is a conceit of the comedy of manners that the best people are the sharpest wits and the subtlest intriguers, and this amoral principle jibed almost exactly with Coward's sense of society's unwritten laws. As a homosexual, he must also have felt an affinity for the genre's disposition to regard the conventions of sexual morality as hollow.

The comedy of manners tends to flourish during periods of high style — the Restoration, the 1890s, the 1920s, the 1960s — and to fall into disrepute during periods of temperamental sobriety. Under the aegis of romantic "sincerity" and Victorian "gloom" in the nineteenth century, the genre was generally considered immoral, a flight from conscience and commitment. Charles Lamb dared to say in its defense, "I am glad for a season to take an airing beyond the diocese of the strict conscience,"[2] but Lord Macaulay complained that the comedy of manners was a forum for "sound morality to be insulted, derided, associated with every thing mean and hateful;

the unsound morality to be set off to every advantage, and inculcated by all methods, direct and indirect."[3] In his influential essay *On the Idea of Comedy and the Uses of the Comic Spirit*, George Meredith defined the genre contemptuously as "the manners of South-Sea islanders under city veneer; and, as to comic idea, vacuous as the mask without the face behind it."[4]

It is against this dark background of nineteenth-century taste that Coward's plays must be seen. His comedies of manners were successful in the gay twenties and the turbulent thirties not only because of their inherent worth as drama but because of a taste for the mannered and the artificial that was a reaction against Victorian seriousness. The same plays were scorned when World War II and the subsequent cold war encouraged more sober modes of expression, cheered again in the 1960s when a taste for high style renewed itself under the sponsorship of Carnaby Street fashions. The audience for comedy of manners seems limited, however, even when the pendulum of taste swings in its favor. The major dramatists of both the seventeenth and the twentieth centuries produced a surprisingly small number of such plays, and Coward wrote only four plays that are generally acknowledged to be comedies of manners: *Hay Fever* (1925), *Private Lives* (1930), *Design for Living* (1933), and *Relative Values* (1951).

Hay Fever

Hay Fever was written in three days upon Coward's return from America in the autumn of 1924 and commemorates Sunday evenings he had spent in New York playing the word game "Adverbs" with the actress Laurette Taylor and her guests. The play was not originally thought well of, either by its author or by the actress Marie Tempest, to whom Coward submitted it as a possible vehicle. He knew certain scenes were good, but he feared the play as a whole was tedious. "I think the reason for this was that I was passing through a transition stage as a writer," he wrote; "my dialogue was becoming more natural and less elaborate, and I was beginning to concentrate more on the comedy values of situation rather than the comedy values of actual lines."[5]

Norman Macdermott expressed an interest in the play for his Everyman Theatre in Hampstead, but Coward persuaded him to produce *The Vortex* instead, since it offered Coward a particularly juicy role. In the wake of *The Vortex's* success, Marie Tempest was approached again and not only found *Hay Fever* charming but insisted Coward direct her in the London production, which he did with trepidation and characteristic flair. They enjoyed a successful run despite qualified reviews. "The press naturally and inevitably described it as 'thin,' 'tenuous,' and 'trivial,'" Coward complained, "because those are their stock phrases for anything later in date and lighter in texture than *The Way of the World*." He could not refrain from pointing out that "it ran, tenuously and triumphantly, for a year."[6]

Hay Fever is a play in three acts about that most venerable of subjects, a weekend house party in a British country home. The gimmick of the play is that each member of the Bliss family has invited a guest without informing the other family members, each promising lodgings in a "Japanese" bedroom that is the best alternative to a room known as Little Hell. Each member of the family has also a vaguely romantic interest in his or her guest. Judith Bliss, a retired actress of extravagant temperament, has invited for the weekend a brawny but dim young man named Sandy Tyrell. Her husband, David, a romantic novelist, has invited a flapper named Jackie Coryton, allegedly for purposes of character study. Their son Simon is a caricaturist and has invited an older woman named Myra Arundel; his sister Sorel has invited Richard Greatham, a diplomat. It is an ill-matched group. The first act ends with the family and guests assembled for Friday afternoon tea, strained nerves all round.

In the second act, the word game "Adverbs" fails to pull the group together on Saturday evening. Bored to the point of impatience with their guests, the family members begin instinctively to improvise a substitute game in which each pretends that a small attention from some other person's guest is a declaration of undying love. This strikes panic in the guests, who find themselves unexpectedly affianced to the wrong persons — Sandy to Sorel, Myra to David, Jackie to Simon, and Richard to Judith. Richard asks if they are playing some sort of game, and Judith answers, "Yes, and a game that must be played to the finish!" Her family recognizes the line, and picking up their cue, they enact a scene from *Love's Whirlwind*, one of Judith's favorite melodramas.

Act III takes place at Sunday morning breakfast, during which the bewildered and emotionally exhausted guests vote to decamp en masse. The Blisses arrive at the table shortly after the decampment, remark upon the bad behavior of the fugitive guests, and shortly discover a new subject on which to exercise their histrionic compulsion. We understand that their behavior is a disease that afflicts vibrant people immured in the country — a kind of "hay fever."

Hay Fever is remarkable for its economy of design. Coward observed that there was no plot and remarkably little action in the play and professed surprise that it was regarded as one of his best works after it was successfully revived by the National Theatre in 1964.[7] His attitude was surely disingenuous, for *Hay Fever*'s economy of method reflects his lifelong taste for clean-lined structures. Though deeply influenced by the nineteenth-century tradition of the well-made play, Coward was in

some ways a modernist. He thought unnecessary twists
of plot messy, disdained visible struts and braces as vulgar, and detested long speeches as Victorian. His impulse
was to temper the well-made play into an Art Deco curve.

Accordingly, *Hay Fever*'s opening scene is a swift
glissade. The curtain goes up on an untidy hall, which
is a visual metaphor for the untidy emotional life of the
household. Simon, in a state of advanced dishevelment,
is crouched on the floor sketching, while Sorel, somewhat better groomed, reads languidly. They discuss an
acquaintance who wrote the book of poetry Sorel is reading, and the expositional aspect of the scene is admirably
efficient. A conflict between bohemian and philistine
sensibilities is established, and an indulgent cynicism
with which the family treats Judith's histrionics is limned.
Coward is also at pains in the scene to ease us into the
play's structure of ironies. Sorel's wish that she were
more "bouncing" looks forward to Judith's "bouncing"
about on the sofa with Sandy; the allusion to games an-
ticipates both the game of Adverbs and the ad hoc game
of betrothals in Act II; and Judith's actressy tapping of
the barometer prefigures a later tapping of the barometer that sends it crashing to the floor, a symbol of atmos-
pheric understanding destroyed.

The scene also introduces a level of verbal and ges-
tural stylization that borders on parody. Phrases such as
"normal and bouncing" and "the Squire's lady" are in-
visibly in inverted commas and lead to such travesties of
upper-class ellipticalness as "Awfully nice place, Cook-
ham," and "This haddock's disgusting."[8] Simon's and
Sorel's remarks about their mother prepare us to understand that all her gestures and many of the gestures she
inspires in her family also border on parody. In Coward's
direction of his plays, he encouraged a stylization of such
ordinary actions as arranging flowers and lighting ciga-
rettes and made them seem deliciously sly takeoffs on the
fashionable world. Practicing the names of the flowers

and tapping the barometer are just such takeoffs on the landed gentry.

The farcical confusion over the Japanese bedroom is so dramaturgically efficient that it cannot finally be played as farce. Although clearly a plot gimmick, the confusion provides a revealing look at Judith's artistic temperament and a first intimation that the family is deeply caught up in her sense of theater. Sorel even observes that an unwritten law of the house requires the family to play up to her mother. If Judith is disconcerted when Sorel first announces that she has promised the Japanese bedroom to Richard, she is more deeply upset when Simon adds his claim for Myra, and when David claims the room for Jackie's use, hysterics seem certain. But after an ominous pause and with a trained sense of understatement, Judith calls for music with the understanding that her family will appreciate that controlled rage needs to be soothed; requests someone — anyone — to play the piano because she has to depend on anonymous charity; asks that the music be played *to her* in order to make clear that she is the most aggrieved party; asks that the music be *very* beautiful in order to convey the ostensible depth of her anguish. She is an actress, not a fishwife.

And so it goes. As Judith glides from scene to scene, willfully exaggerating the significance of a kiss here, an embrace there, the line of action is smoothly uncluttered, a sinuous drift of her histrionic imagination. What appears to the guests to be madness is a gathering of her past performances that reaches a climax at the end of Act II, when the whole family joins her in the scene from *Love's Whirlwind*. Parody is the keynote of these scenes, and the overwrought emotions of Victorian and Edwardian melodrama are their satiric focus.

The four guests are basically foils for the stylish histrionics of the Blisses. Bromidic, unoriginal, sluggish of mind and temperament, they marshal platitudes while their hosts strike attitudes. Typically, the conversational repertoire of Jackie and Richard is nearly exhausted by observations that Italy is nice, Rome beautiful, Capri enchanting, and Dieppe dear — and as their repertoire runs dry, they speculate anxiously on whether the unconventional Blisses will serve tea at the appointed hour. Coward was always skillful in conveying the desperation of persons barely able to sustain conversation, and there is no finer demonstration of that skill than in the exchanges between Jackie and Richard.

It is Coward's fundamental joke that the Blisses are the true realists in the play despite their histrionic emotions. With evident pride in her candor, Myra confesses that she accepted Simon's invitation only in order to meet his father David, the distinguished author of romantic novels. When David suggests that she flatters him because she wants to stage an affair, Myra is conventionally outraged, but partly because David has upstaged her pretense of candor. He protests that he seems annoying only because he likes first to see things for what they are and then to affect that they are something other. "Words!" cries Myra, but she misjudges David and his family if she means that their verbal games have no foundation in reality. The Blisses can mock the conventional emotions with equanimity and play variations up and down the emotional scale because they accept a basic truth their guests do not: that all human behavior is compounded of such imitations, consciously or unconsciously.

Even Sorel's observation that the Blisses never mean anything by what they do or say is not fair to the family, for it discounts the occasional subtext. When Judith catches her husband in Myra's arms, she elects to play the scene with dignity. But David counters her arch request to forgive the interruption by asking if there are any chocolates in the house. She continues to take a high tone, and he continues to murmur that, really, he would like nothing better than a chocolate. In the subtext of the

scene, David is not just playing at comic inconsequence
but telling his wife that Myra leaves him hungry and that
their embrace was nothing more than a passing desire
for sweets. The subtextual reassurance allows Judith to
play her scene for theatrics alone, and when David joins
in the scene, he is indulging her lovingly by alleging his
love for Myra. Only Myra loses her sense of reality in the
scene. She is too busy protesting the facts of the situation to see things as they are.

One of the most effective bits of dramaturgy in *Hay
Fever* is the Blisses' ability to shift as abruptly into perfect
frankness as into any other emotional key. When Simon
asks Judith what they are to do about their awkward
assembly of guests, Judith composes a motherly tableau,
pulling him to his knees and placing his head on her right
shoulder (Sorel's head on her left) and murmuring sweetly
that they must be kind to everyone. But Simon is im-
pervious to Judith's effects and objects to her performance. He even points out that she was never really beautiful on stage — which remark inspires Judith not to rage
but to the dispassionate, professional observation that she
managed to make audiences *think* she was. Her announcement that she will resume her career is the same
sort of scene, startling not for its factual revelations but
for Judith's honesty about her motive. When Sorel suggests that she retired so very finally the year before and
enquires what excuse might be given for a precipitous
return to the boards, Judith points unabashedly to letters
from her public as the decisive factor — not to an ava-
lanche of fan mail but to the one or two letters that
should have been hundreds.

Such frankness is more than a parody of the family's
affectation of perfect frankness, although it is that, too.
David's expostulation that both his children should be
in reformatories and Judith's memorable complaint that
Sorel is less a good daughter to her than a critical *aunt*
set the tone for Sorel's easy recognition that she is not a

good hostess and for Judith's recognition that she is not and never was beautiful. What the play illumines is a paradox in which only those who play at frankness can be frank and only those who play at emotions can feel deeply. In a moment of high dudgeon, Myra says the house is a feather bed of false emotions, but her image defeats her invective. Feather beds are commodious and comfortable environments, and the family is extraordinarily at ease with true as well as with false feeling. Even Sorel forgets her wistful yearnings for a more conventional life whenever family scenes offer her a good part. Myra complains of being overwhelmed by theatrical effects in the household, but those theatrical effects betoken an animation of mind and feeling in the Blisses that makes Myra and her kind seem moribund.

Hay Fever has proven durable on the stage partly because of this mock-serious defense of the theatrical temperament, but in life Coward was less tolerant of theatrical egotists and rather disliked the 1920s cult of bad manners that Hay Fever did something to encourage. For those reasons, perhaps, the last act of Hay Fever ends with uncharacteristically heavy irony as the Blisses criticize their guests' rudeness in departing abruptly — as if they had no insight into the comedy of bad manners they themselves have staged relentlessly. There is a marked tiredness about the third act, and a whiff of déjà vu clings to comic routines dulled by repetition. Judith wants to cry when she remembers her children in their perambulators until Sorel points out she never saw them in their perambulators, to which fact Judith readily assents — but too familiarly at that point and not comically enough.

This third-act heaviness is a curious failing of a successful play, and one wonders if Coward feared that his comedy of manners had grown too tolerant of bad manners. "I had been brought up by Mother in the tradition of good manners," he once pointed out.[9] It was perhaps an enduring sense of obligation to good manners that made him withdraw a measure of sympathy from the Blisses in the last act, jeopardizing the play's tone and trivializing its fine insouciance.

Private Lives

Private Lives was written in 1929 as a vehicle for Gertrude Lawrence. Coward had promised Lawrence the role of Sari in *Bitter Sweet*, but when the score for that operetta was complete, both she and Coward realized that her voice was not strong enough for the demanding music. As he departed on a world cruise after the New York première of *Bitter Sweet*, he promised her that his next play would be for her. The idea for *Private Lives* came to him in December 1929 in a hotel room in Tokyo: "The moment I switched out the lights, Gertie appeared in a white Molyneux dress on a terrace in the South of France and refused to go again until four a.m., by which time *Private Lives*, title and all, had constructed itself."[10] A few months later, he wrote the play in four days, and by February it was typed, revised, and ready for production. "In 1923 the play would have been written and typed within a few days of my thinking of it," he observed, "but in 1929 I had learned the wisdom of not welcoming a new idea too ardently, so I forced it into the back of my mind, trusting to its own integrity to emerge again later on, when it had become sufficiently set and matured."[11]

Private Lives is based on elaborate coincidences. Elyot Chase and Amanda Prynne, who have been divorced from each other for five years, find themselves in adjacent hotel suites on the night each is beginning a honeymoon with a second spouse. Horrified by the situation, Elyot tells his young wife they must leave because he has a strange foreboding, while Amanda admits to her new husband that she has seen Elyot in the distance and insists they move to another hotel. Both spouses refuse to indulge what they consider hysterical nonsense, and the inevitable happens: fresh from the first quarrel of their new marriages, Elyot and Amanda fall into each other's arms and decide to run away together at once. Act I ends with the spouses, Victor and Sibyl, meeting each other and toasting absent friends.

Act II takes place a week later in a Paris flat, where Elyot and Amanda punctuate their unwedded bliss with quarrels of the headstrong sort that had destroyed their marriage years before. They have kept their quarrels in check thus far by observing five minutes of silence when either cries "sollocks," but this argument-stopping device is finally insufficient to restrain them, and they erupt into physical violence. Victor and Sibyl discover the love nest of their spouses just in time to catch them wrestling on the floor, knocking tables and lamps about in their rage.

Act III takes place the next morning and contains a number of heated exchanges, after which Elyot and Amanda agree to the divorces insisted upon by Sibyl and Victor. Their tempers cooled, Elyot and Amanda begin to charm one another anew, but their spouses become increasingly disputatious. The play ends with Sibyl and Victor trading insults and finally blows as Elyot and Amanda exit together, suitcases in hand.

Symmetry is the first and most distinctive note struck by *Private Lives*. The opening mise-en-scène is elaborately symmetrical and is usually given a mathematically precise character in production, with matching terraces, corresponding sets of French doors, identical furnishings, and a line of tubbed plants bisecting the stage as precisely as a plumb line. The dialogue and physical movement of the characters are almost as neatly balanced. Sibyl steps onto the terrace and calls to Elyot to come admire the view. Victor makes the same entrance a few minutes later, calling to Amanda in nearly the same words as Elyot from the other side of the terrace. In her newlywed's anxiety, Sibyl questions Elyot about his marriage to Amanda. Was his first wife prettier than she? Did she dance better? Elyot's remarks about his first wife tend toward a balance that resonates with the balance of the stage settings. Rejecting Sibyl's suggestion that Amanda was to blame for the failure of their marriage, he insists that they made each *other* miserable and that they lost each *other*. Minutes later, Victor probes the happiness of Amanda's first marriage in a similar way, and Amanda strikes the same note of balance as Elyot, insisting upon a shared responsibility for their divorce.

Such neat correspondences proliferate and tend to cut across the new marriages, aligning Elyot with Amanda, Victor with Sibyl. Elyot and Amanda both want to acquire a sunburn, while both Victor and Sibyl say they hate sunburned women. Elyot and Amanda both look forward to the gambling tables, while Victor and Sibyl are surprised and vaguely scandalized that their spouses have the gaming passion. Thinking of his new marriage, Elyot hopes it will be cosy and undramatic; pressed by Victor to say that her love for him is different from her love for Elyot, Amanda says she loves him more calmly, if that's what he means. And when their respective spouses refuse to leave with them instantly, Elyot and Amanda turn ugly in identical ways. Clearly, the new marriages are mésalliances, not just because they come apart so easily, but because Amanda and Elyot are evenly matched in the play's system of balances.

A tendency of *Private Lives* to play as farce helps to explain these symmetries. From the medieval miracle plays to the Marx Brothers, farce deals with an improbable situation in which the forces of reason and convention contend with sweetly anarchic unreason. The representatives of unreason rebel in such a way as to disrupt

civilized dignity but not in such a way as to make a sa-
tirical comment. The genre avoids social criticism by
creating a world so artificial, so stylized and mechanical,
that the everyday world is never really its subject. Indeed, the characters and values that are attacked by the
forces of unreason usually resume their conventionally
dominant roles when unreason's revolt is over.

Private Lives is farcical in this mode and to this
degree. The extravagant symmetries of the play extenu-
ate Elyot's and Amanda's revolts against propriety, and
the clockwork mechanism of exits and entrances, timed
so that one pair of characters exits as another enters, is
the sort of shapeliness that suggests an ultimate order
able to subsume fisticuffs as easily as a decree nisi. Victor
and Sibyl represent convention until the reversal at the
end of the third act.

As part of its tendency to slip into farce, *Private
Lives* also tends to slip into the form of childhood games —
notably hide-and-seek. Elyot recommends that he and
Amanda run from Victor and Sibyl and so they flee to
free-thinking Paris, where they hide from their spouses
in Amanda's flat and wait to be caught. When Sibyl and
Victor succeed in finding them, Amanda plays "house,"
apologizing for the untidiness of the wrecked living room
and ordering coffee and rolls, while Elyot plays ostrich,
shutting his bedroom door and refusing to see Victor and
Sibyl. Extending this game metaphor, Elyot remarks of
Amanda's charade that they will shortly be playing Hunt
the Slipper, apparently seeing himself both as the slipper
passed from person to person and as the owner of the
slipper, who must try to regain it.

This is not to say that *Private Lives* is a farce but
only that it edges near to the genre. Farce is by definition
unsophisticated: it is "comedy with the meaning left
out,"[12] "comedy with *self-awareness* left out."[13] Elyot
and Amanda are intensely self-aware and so sophisticated that they find it hard to pretend the innocence

their spouses expect of them. When Victor refers to
Amanda as a child, she points out that her heart is
steeped in sophistication and that she has always been
far too knowing. To Victor's shock, she suspects that she
is abnormal deep down in her private life, and she knows
she is unreliable and apt to perceive things the wrong
way. Similarly, Elyot knows himself to be frivolous, and
he believes in his frivolity as in a sacred trust. One
mustn't be serious, he tells Amanda, for it's just what the
moralists want. One must laugh and be flippant and
leave the moralists to their acidic view of things.

Their amicably divorced relationship also gives
Elyot and Amanda an aura of sophistication. The divorce rate increased dramatically in England after the
first World War, and it increased steadily by as much
as 50 percent a year through the 1920s as divorce gained
acceptability. Coward's autobiography records a phenomenon of Ivor Novello's parties in the 1920s — that
divorced couples were to be seen hobnobbing with each
other and with each other's corespondents.[14] Such conduct was increasingly fashionable in cultivated circles
but was still exceptional enough in 1930 to signal sophisticated behavior in a comedy of manners.

The farcical elements of *Private Lives* function as
a point of reference for such sophistication, defining its
limits and suggesting that farce lurks under the comedy
of manners like trolls under a bridge. In accordance with
the laws of farce, the sophistication of Elyot and Amanda
takes a number of pratfalls: their suavity runs aground
on old jealousies, and their glib repartee turns more than
once into the squabbling of willful children. Elyot takes
a notable fall when he says his flippancy is designed to
bring out the acid in moralists, for we recall that Amanda
has previously compared the two of them to acids in a
matrimonial bottle. Does a moralist, then, lurk deep in
Elyot's disdain for all that is right, decent, and tradi-
tional? Amanda catches him out when she admits to hav-

ing been promiscuous during their years apart, and he protests that it doesn't suit the character of women to be promiscuous. "It doesn't suit men for women to be promiscuous," Amanda fires back.

It is because Elyot and Amanda live on the brink of farce that their verbal sophistication involves such a large measure of silliness. The most charming moments of the play transpire when they pretend to be boring and conventional, teasing the moment with banalities. A reluctance to allude in any way to the breakup of their marriage inspires them to remark with arch irrelevance upon the bigness of China and the smallness of Japan. Their pretense of religious and social sensitivities is outrageously camp, as innocent of seriousness as of consequence. Amanda affects concern that they are living in sin, and Elyot reassures her that Catholics, not believing in divorce, consider their original marriage intact in the eyes of heaven. But Amanda alleges a somewhat greater concern with the eyes of society—with which, of course, she is not really concerned at all.

Their breezy cross talk would lose a measure of its effect if Amanda and Elyot did not live on the edge of farce, where banter can turn physically aggressive at any moment. Irritated by Elyot's refusal to take seriously her affectation of a social manner, Amanda announces that she considers it unmannerly for a man to strike a woman—in response to which Elyot remarks famously that some women should be struck as regularly as gongs. The fatuity of the simile is half farcical, half self-mockery, an altogether engaging mix that positions Elyot within the comedy of manners but just barely. He has the opportunity to step into farce simply by implementing his theory of women, and that possibility is salt to the scene.

Dramaturgically, *Private Lives* is very little more than a sequence of such stylized exchanges. Yet it is an eminently theatrical play. Its dialogue is textured by an extraordinary mix of tones—disenchantment, wry hu-

mor, arrant sentimentalism, ennui, whimsy. We have
sad statements that things are horribly funny, *dispassionate* scenes of utter rage, *cheerful* predictions of di-
saster. Hybrid emotions are the norm. Elyot remarks that
a tune is "nasty" to prove that he is deeply moved when
the orchestra plays a favorite melody he associates with
Amanda and his first honeymoon. Amanda looks particularly lovely in the "damned" moonlight, he tells her,
loath to trust his sentiment to such a conventional stimu-
lant as moonlight.

Innumerable shifts in tone and this tendency of the
main characters to express themselves obliquely impart
to the play a sense of movement that belies its lack of
dramatic action. Coward had an actor's sense of how a
scene should play, and he built a scene less from ideas
and statements than from rhythms of exchange, from a
counterpoint of moods, and from twists and turns of
rhetoric that convey the nervous vitality of his characters. The third-act scene in which Amanda summons her
most gracious manner to preside at a breakfast with
Elyot, Sibyl, and Victor is typical of the play and typically masterful. Amanda's concern for passing sugar and
milk pointedly omits Elyot and favors the witless Victor.
A game of one-upmanship between Amanda and Sibyl
is an undercurrent of the dialogue, and Victor is mindlessly ill at ease, like a dog sensitive to tension in the air
without understanding its source. And yet the scene is
nothing but a sharing of morning coffee — its ordinariness
a counterpoint to the extraordinary array of temperaments that threatens to dissolve the ceremony of cups and
saucers into open hostilities. The genius of the scene is
its tempo — a retard on the cut and thrust of the dialogue
that makes portentous developments wait upon the rit-
uals of morning coffee.

The ending of the play is unexpected but somehow
inevitable. Having run the course of their quarrel, Elyot
and Amanda find their attraction for one another well-

ing up again. Soon Amanda has to choke back the laughter that Elyot's irrespressibility can always induce. Victor turns on Elyot angrily as Amanda chokes on her laughter, and Sibyl springs to Elyot's defense, slapping Victor's face as he shakes her by the shoulders. Amanda and Elyot depart with smiles, presumably en route to a new love nest. This final tableau announces the triumph of frivolity: the demon of temper in Amanda and Elyot has relocated itself in Sibyl and Victor, and Elyot and Amanda take their leave as innocent of involvement in the quarrel as of concern for their spouses. It is an audacious vision — farcically symmetrical but too morally ambiguous for farce, exactly suited to a comedy of manners that proclaims contemporary manners *are* a farce. Victor's and Sibyl's quarrel actually gives us hope for them, for their bad behavior is a measure of their potential for loving one another in Coward's emotionally symmetric world.

Design for Living

Design for Living was written as a showpiece for the combined talents of Coward and the Lunts. It was informally contracted for in 1921, when Alfred Lunt and Lynn Fontanne, not yet married, became fast friends with Coward while the three were living in the same theatrical boarding house in New York City's West Seventies. Full of delicatessen potato salad, dill pickles, and bravado, they sketched one evening an agenda for their nascent careers that was remarkably prophetic:

Lynn and Alfred were to be married. That was the first plan. Then they were to become definitely idols of the public. That was the second plan. Then, all this being successfully accomplished, they were to act exclusively together. This was the third plan. It remained for me to supply the fourth, which was that when all three of us had become stars of sufficient magnitude to be able to count upon an individual following irrespective of each other, then, poised serenely upon that enviable plane of achievement, we would meet and act triumphantly together.[15]

Eleven years later, the Lunts reminded Coward of the plan in a telegram that tracked him to Chile, where he was vacationing:

OUR CONTRACT WITH THEATRE GUILD UP IN JUNE WHAT ABOUT IT?[16]

Coward lost no time in setting to work. The formidable challenge of writing a play for three stars of equal magnitude was transformed into a play about three creative people functioning in off-again, on-again tandem, and the play opened in New York in January 1933 to rave notices. Reviewing the play in *The New York Times*, Brooks Atkinson recognized it for what it is: "an actors' lark" written for "an incomparable trio of high comedians."[17]

In the first act of *Design for Living*, a dealer in pictures named Ernest Friedman arrives at the Paris studio of his friend, the painter Otto Sylvus. The door is opened by Gilda, an interior decorator with whom Otto lives, and she tells Ernest that Otto is still asleep in the bedroom. Ernest mentions that a mutual friend, the playwright Leo Mercuré, has returned from America and is staying at a local hotel. When Otto bursts into the room, not from the bedroom but just back from Bordeaux, he is sent off with Ernest to visit Leo and bring him back for the day. Leo then emerges from the bedroom, where he has obviously spent the night. He and Gilda discuss their quandary—that they love each other *and* Otto, as he loves both of them. Otto returns, realizes the situation, and storms out of the studio damning them both to hell.

Act II discovers Leo and Gilda living together in Leo's London flat eighteen months later. Leo is the author of a new hit play and is sought after by hostesses and newspaper interviewers, much to his delight. Gilda finds something missing in their lives — Otto, of course — and when he arrives abruptly at their door, she falls into his arms, and he, into her bed. Otto thinks the situation of Act I has been reversed and that Leo is now the odd man out, but Gilda shocks her paramours when she abruptly leaves them both.

Act III finds Gilda two years later, ensconced as Mrs. Ernest Friedman in a luxurious New York apartment. A stage note suggests that she is more composed than before, but her vitality appears less. Otto and Leo arrive together in the middle of a small cocktail gathering and drive out the guests with their extravagantly fey conversation. Gilda insists they leave too, to avoid scandal, but she slips them a passkey and then takes to her heels in nearly blind panic. Ernest returns from a business trip the next morning and finds Otto and Leo in his pajamas and dressing gowns, and Gilda gone. They explain quite frankly that they want Gilda back and predict that she will return to the apartment shortly. Gilda does return and confesses they are right, that she is going to leave Ernest because she cannot possibly live without them. The play ends with Ernest storming out of the room in a fury and tripping over a stack of canvases as Gilda, Otto, and Leo roar with laughter.

With its profusion of exits and entrances and its revolving door alliances, *Design for Living* owes a debt to the tradition of farce, like *Private Lives* before it. A servant named Hodge is classically farcical in her complete dishevelment, her wildly erratic *h*'s, and her understandable confusion about the sexual goings-on. When Leo and Otto are introduced to Henry and Helen Carver at Gilda's cocktail party, farce suspends the action of the play and permits a charming regression to nonsense. Leo asks if the Carvers have ever visited Chuquicamata, a copper mine in Chile, and he affects a lofty disdain when they confess they have not. Mr. Carver is made increasingly angry by Leo's supercilious manner, and his wife increasingly nervous. The situation builds explosively until Leo and Otto observe blithely that they too have never visited Chuquicamata — and the elaborate, quite unnecessary show of temperaments is suddenly rendered farcical.

But such farcical moments are less typical of *Design for Living* than moments of ideological and moral pronouncement that render the play more sober in tone than both *Private Lives* and *Hay Fever*. Ernest asks Gilda in the first act if there is any reason why she doesn't marry Otto, and she replies that there is a very good reason — that she loves him too much to bind him to her legally. Her statement is unqualified by humor or irony, with the result that it falls heavily upon the ear expecting Cowardly insouciance. Sending Otto to bring Leo back from his hotel and knowing that he will shortly have to face himself betrayed, she strikes a motherly note, cautioning him to be careful crossing roads, to look right and left and all around, and not to do anything foolish or impulsive. In another mood, she exclaims that she looks upon her own "damn" femininity with nausea. We wait in vain for a joke that will prove her feminine angst spurious. Otto and Leo are less consistently solemn than Gilda, but they too deal in profundities unrelieved by wit and argue bromidically that love is not mathematics and that principles should be adhered to.

The themes of the play are characterized by a similar drift toward solemnity. Gilda's reluctance to submerge herself in the successes of Otto and Leo is entirely serious, as is her distaste for using feminine blandishments to gain any measure of personal success. The ménage à trois projected at the last curtain promises connatural satisfactions, not indiscriminate coupling, and there is nothing comically salacious or light-minded about it, despite its reputation. Gilda's fear that commercial

success will compromise Leo and Otto is not idle roman-
ticism, any more than Leo's refusal to shut out the world
and live for art alone is hedonism. All three of the pro-
tagonists are hard workers and do not lend themselves
to caricature as dilettantes or adventurers. In short, life
among the artists is a surprisingly solemn affair in *Design
for Living*. Flippant allusions to "Love among the Artists"
adorn the play but do not obscure its underlying seriousness.

A critic for *The Times* noted this mixture of seriousness and flippancy in the play and suggested, "It is not
a question only of mixing conventions; it is almost a question of running away."[18] If there is something evasive
about Coward's technique in the play, it is possibly because he himself dwelt comfortably in a ménage and because he believed too firmly in enjoying his own success
to make fun of Otto's and Leo's pleasure in having made
their fortunes. It is not clear in the play that Otto and
Leo are lovers, but it is clear that they were friends before Gilda entered their lives, and when they return to
her after her marriage, they project an intimacy with
each other more intense than their intimacy with her.
The relationship of Otto, Leo, and Gilda is too psycho-
dynamically complex to be simply a mask, but the evident intimacy of the two men and their cultivation of
Gilda may have suggested to Coward a ruse of the homosexual celebrity that he had no wish to parody.[19]

Gilda's desire to live a conventional life should have
been the central joke of the play, but it is played more
for drama than for laughs. Leo asks wistfully in Act II
if the three of them will ever live together again, and
Gilda answers vehemently that she has no wish to recon-
stitute the ménage à trois. But why is she so vehement?
It is by no means clear that Leo implies a sexual to-
getherness, and it is not clear why Gilda should object
to such an arrangement even if he did. Her difficulty in
living first with Otto and then with Leo seems to be her

feminist urge to match their commercial success as artists with a success of her own — a success she achieves while married to Ernest and which leaves her empty. A charge of running away from a biological destiny as wife and mother hangs unaccountably over Gilda as a result and explains her lapse into motherly solicitude when she is preparing to leave Otto. Indeed, her marriage to the older and distinctly paternal Ernest seems an oblique attempt both to satisfy and to evade the biological call.

But the larger question of the play is on what basis Gilda, Otto, and Leo should form an inevitable grouping. Because Gilda is in flight from one or both of her two men until the last minutes of the play, the three are never seen to amuse each other so intensely that their unconventional relationship is justified — which is the usual logic of Coward's plays. Wit and intelligence do not distinguish the three as a unit, and so they do not rise above those around them as ineffably as Elyot, Amanda, and the Blisses. One is not even convinced that Gilda is the equal of Otto and Leo, inasmuch as she is neither successful nor particularly talented as an interior decorator. She makes her mark as a merchandiser of fine objects, but that ranks her spiritually and temperamentally with Ernest.

The laughter on which the final curtain descends underscores these equivocations of the play, inasmuch as audiences tend to be unsure whether they should join in the laughter. Coward himself recognized the difficulty:

The three of them, after various partings and reunions and partings again, after torturing and loving and hating one another, are left together as the curtain falls, laughing. Different minds found different meanings in this laughter. Some considered it to be directed against Ernest, Gilda's husband, and the time-honoured friend of all three. If so, it was certainly cruel, and in the worst possible taste. Some saw in it a lascivious anticipation of a sort of triangular carnal frolic. Others, with less ribald imaginations, regarded it as a meaningless and slightly inept excuse to bring the curtain down. I as author, however, prefer to think that Gilda and Otto and Leo were laughing at themselves.[20]

It is not enough to say they are laughing at themselves, because Gilda, at least, has not generally found their situation humorous. Her laughter might better be played as hysterical release — a nervous, final relaxation into her fate.

Fate is important as a concept in *Design for Living*, for in the last analysis the play celebrates the irrationalism of human bonding, its victories over feminist sensitivities, the marriage contract, and heterosexual orthodoxy. Gilda, Otto, and Leo are helpless to oppose their fated union, and their jealousies and betrayals fall like ninepins before the force that draws them together. Their attraction to each other is simply ordained — a dramaturgical fate. Numerous statements in the text draw attention to that fact. Everything is glandular, Gilda opines at the beginning of the play. Chance drew the three of them together and tied their lives into a knot, says Otto in Act II. The three of them are finally of a piece, says Gilda at the end.

The best scenes in the play suggest this triumph of an irrational bond over the characters' various designs for living. The scene in which Gilda says goodbye to Otto with real affection, unhappy to leave him for Leo, is especially successful because of its stratified, irreconcilable emotions. The scene at the end of Act II in which Leo and Otto get drunk together as their coin of tribute to anarchy is beautifully paced and inveterately a crowd pleaser. Since conventional thinking condemns the relationship of the three main characters, silliness is the idiom in which they best express their affection. Inconsequence has rarely limned affection so well as when Otto arrives to upset Leo's love nest and Gilda welcomes him nervously, but with a sense of relief.

Such scenes make *Design for Living* a comedy of
linguistic manners as well as of cohabitational mores,
and it is for its comedy that the play survives. In a
famous line, Gilda observes that Ernest has referred to
her as both a jaguar and an ox and expresses the wish
that he would be less zoological. The wit is typically
Coward's — brash, brittle, situational rather than epi-
grammatic. The American drama critic George Jean
Nathan objected to the line on the basis of its vaude-
villian antecedent ("So I'm a goat and a jackass, huh?
You talk like you was in a zoo!"), but he failed to appreciate Coward's reworking of the joke, in which mo-
ronic aggression becomes a camp non sequitur, and the
uninspired juncture of "goat," "jackass," and "zoo" becomes a play of the archly precise "zoological" against
the exotic "jaguar" and the homely "ox."[21] Such honed
lines are not adequate to relieve the burden of solemnity
in the play, but *Design for Living* still commands British
and American stages because of the sophisticated shim-
mer they impart.

Relative Values

The idea for *Relative Values* came to Coward as most
of the ideas for his plays, in a flash. The day of illumination was March 23, 1951 — a Good Friday Coward
described in his diaries as a *very* Good Friday.[22] Reviews that accused Coward of old-fashioned theatrics
had prompted him to concentrate on prose fiction for
several months, and he resumed playwriting with relief.
"The flow is beginning," he wrote in his diary on March
26, "and oh, the bliss of writing dialogue after prose."[23]
Relative Values began rehearsals in September with
Gladys Cooper and Angela Baddeley in the leading roles,
and though Cooper had only a shaky command of her
lines, it opened in London on November 28, 1951, to
rave reviews.

Relative Values takes place in the family living room of Marshwood House, East Kent. In the first act it is announced that Nigel, the young Earl of Marshwood, is affianced to Miranda Frayle, an American film star. Felicity, the dowager countess of Marshwood, tries to be philosophical. It is not the first marriage between an actress and a peer of the realm, she observes. The butler Crestwell is as unflappable about the coming nuptials as about all things, but Moxie, Felicity's personal maid, is deeply distressed and mutters darkly that she will walk out when Miranda walks in. Pressed by the countess to give her real reason for leaving Marshwood House, Moxie confesses that Miranda Frayle is her sister. What to do about such a socially impossible situation? The Honorable Peter Ingleton, Felicity's nephew, suggests that Moxie be promoted to secretary-companion, but Crestwell observes that she would still be socially inferior to her sister. He suggests they pretend she has come into an inheritance and is now a resident friend of the family. With profound misgivings, Moxie agrees to the deception, since Miranda is not apt to recognize a sister she has not seen for twenty-five years.

In the second act, Nigel is all nerves upon introducing his future wife to the household. Miranda plays at being the simple, unaffected type, choosing lemonade rather than a martini, carrying needlework about with her, and gushing sentimentally about her new English home. She also affects to have had a disadvantaged childhood, a fantasy that incenses Moxie. The situation becomes melodramatic when Don Lucas arrives in pursuit of Miranda, whom he has loved notoriously both on- and offscreen. With a flash of inspiration, Felicity insists he spend the night, and in reaction Nigel announces peremptorily that he and Miranda will be married in the morning. Moxie then reveals abruptly that Miranda is her wayward sister.

Act III takes place the next morning. Both Moxie and Miranda have announced they are quitting the

house, and Felicity increases Miranda's prospects of unhappiness by announcing she will be a resident mother-
in-law at Marshwood and will require that Moxie remain
on the staff. All this has the desired effect of throwing
Miranda into Don Lucas's waiting arms — a development
that suddenly suits Nigel, who has no taste for histrionics.
The play ends with tranquillity reestablished, Miranda
and Don Lucas fled, and Felicity hustling everyone off
to church.

Like *Hay Fever*, *Relative Values* mixes the world
of the theater and the world of the English country
house. Miranda plays at being sweet and demure among
chintzes in the family sitting room, while fan magazines
like *Screenland* and *Photoplay* bestrew the servants' bed-
rooms, and girl guides seeking autographs lurk in the
shrubbery. Conversely, Moxie worries about making an
exhibition of herself in front of the other servants by
pretending to be gentry. The mix of two such different
attitudes is a durable formula for a comedic clash of
manners, and Crestwell points up the antecedents of the
play when he suggests that the coincidental meeting of
the two sisters is in the best traditions of English High
Comedy. He even invites us to consider how Somerset
Maugham would have developed the situation.

With a fine sense of the outré, Coward strikes sparks
from the clash of Hollywood and country-house manners. Miranda irritates everyone by affecting Goody Two-
shoes innocence and choosing lemonade over the Martini that Felicity considers a more healthy drink. Don
Lucas is crassly American, addressing Felicity as "Ma'am"
and Crestwell as "Fred." By some inexplicable Hollywood vulgarity, Miranda and Lucas address each other
(and occasionally others) as "Pete." "Ma'am" is a vaguely
royal appelation, Felicity objects, but Lucas's stumbling
alternative, "Ma'am — Felicity," is worse, evoking for
Felicity's ear the infelicitous "Grandma Moses" or "Mother Goddam." American speech habits are not only in-

elegant but confusing to the Marshwood ear, as when Lucas says he is going to play a "bum" in his next picture and Felicity tries to imagine an anatomical impersonation. Crestwell assumes his most starched manner when dealing with American syntax, and in his initial interview with Lucas he overwhelms the monosyllabic American with calculated prolixity.

Like American vulgarity, Moxie's elevation from lady's maid to friend-of-the-family tests the mettle of country-house manners. Though he has agreed to treat Moxie as a social equal, Nigel winces when she asks to be served a drink, and Felicity blanches when Lady Cynthia Hayling, who has not been told of Moxie's new status, blithely asks her to mend a torn handbag during dinner and is told in response that she will be forgetting her head next. The code of manners among the servants also has its comic turns, from Moxie's use of Crestwell's first name as a signal she is angry with him to Crestwell's habit of insulting the housemaids with such erudition that they barely understand their offenses.

But underneath such standard comedy-of-manners fare runs a serious concern with the mystique of social equality. It is amusing that servants are the first to object to Nigel's intention to marry outside his class, but allusions to villagers who reject domestic service as common and cap and apron as the garb of slavery align the Marshwood servants with a lost social order. Moxie's most ready objection to Nigel's marriage is that he is betraying his class, but because we sense deeper, more personal objections in her from the first, her notions of class seem irrelevant to real experience. Crestwell is the most eloquent of the servants in criticizing the breakdown of England's class structure, but he is so dispassionately witty and precise that his position seems more affected than considered. He defines social equality as a belief that all menial work should be done by someone else. He announces sardonically that Moxie's sudden elevation is a social experiment based on the curious notion that, as we are equal in the eyes of God, we should also be equal in the eyes of our fellow men. Utopia, he says, is a hygienic abstraction wherein everyone is hailed familiarly and there is no domestic service. Utopia sounds invidiously like the America of Don and Miranda, where everyone is "Pete."

The upper classes are predictably supportive of class distinctions but more sensitive than the servants to the republican spirit of the age. Lady Hayling acknowledges that social barriers are being swept away and that any suggestion of class distinction is de trop, but she dislikes creeping egalitarianism. Peter is a realist about social distinctions and tends toward random accommodations. He points out that Felicity might take her golf instructor to the ballet but not her butler — who, in any case, considers the ballet decadent. Nigel is willing to brave the indignity of an unseen Aunt Rose by marrying a Hollywood actress, but he worries what that standard-bearing aunt will think about Moxie being entertained in the drawing room.

Felicity is less double-minded than those around her. She tries to be receptive to her son's marriage and argues that peers of the realm have always amused themselves by marrying actresses. When Peter presses the point, she confesses that she would be happier if Nigel married someone of his own class, but she is genuinely shocked to realize that she doesn't know Moxie half as well as Moxie knows her — that only once in nineteen years of association has she ever seen Moxie in a dressing gown. Knowledge of character does not necessarily depend on seeing people in their dressing-gowns, Peter suggests lightly, but he cannot dispel Felicity's embarrassed realization that she has kept Moxie at a distance. Like Coward himself, Felicity is egocentric in a way that seems to her not morally tenable.

Felicity's wit is an effective gauge of her moral centricity. It is not Crestwell's humor — brittle, crafted, and somewhat cruel — but a humor that uses candor to undercut all codes of manners. When Felicity tells Nigel she plans to leave Marshwood to give Miranda a clear field and Nigel objects that she got along all right with Joan, his first wife, Felicity is charmingly straightforward in her observation that getting along with Joan was one of the more spectacular achievements of her life. Nigel rejoins platitudinously that Miranda is really simple and sweet, quite unlike her screen personality, and Felicity's response springs from a precise sense of her experience: she has seen her at the cinema as a hospital nurse, a gangster's moll, a nun, and Catherine the Great, she observes, so it is difficult for her to form a definite opinion. Felicity is also a master of the disingenuous riposte and refuses to be forced into false positions. She gives Miranda every benefit of the doubt, she assures Nigel — of very *grave* doubts. Miranda insists that she is not as stupid as Felicity thinks, and Felicity responds airily that she is relieved. They have nothing further to say to each other, Miranda finally explodes, and Felicity expresses fear for their long winter evenings together and proposes the purchase of a television set.

This is not to say that Felicity is herself unmannered and that *Relative Values* counterpoises natural and affected behavior. Felicity is accomplished at playing understatement against overstatement for comic effect, and she knows how to deflate grandiloquence with irrelevance, as when she squelches one of Lady Hayling's outbursts by protesting that righteous indignation should not be permitted to take freedoms with syntax. Her manipulation of Don Lucas's presence is almost too adroit, but it ensures our recognition that her candor is disingenuous, as much a manner as Nigel's amateur galumphing, Crestwell's aloofness, Miranda's needlework, and Lucas's flourish of manhood. Her moral centricity to the play is based not on being innocent of manner but on the cultivation of a manner that accommodates her kindness without compromising her intelligence and that allows the truth to be stated without equivocation.

Felicity's concern with her responsibility to the village also bears on her moral centricity. Nigel spurns all obligations to the village; Miranda sees the village only as a setting for her latest role; and the higher-ranking servants, though conscious of a need to consider the village, look down on the locals for looking down on them. Only Felicity speaks up for social obligation. She insists that old Mrs. Willis's son be given an interview for his newspaper because Mrs. Willis supports the Cottage Hospital Committee, and she argues that little Elsie Mumby can't be dismissed from the shrubbery as if she were *any* girl guide inasmuch as she enjoys local sainthood for having pulled her younger brother from a well. When Felicity insists that Don Lucas stay the night, she obviously hopes that he will steal Miranda from Nigel, but habitual consideration of social duty prompts her to add that the villagers will rise up and stone her if she lets him depart unseen. At the end of the play she waves Miranda and Don Lucas off to London and clucks the others off to the village church, that most central of country institutions, worrying because the last bell has rung and that they are already late. They must try to look as though nothing has happened, she enjoins, because, after all, nothing much has.

If nothing much has happened, it is because Felicity is felicitously triumphant. The servants are restored to their accustomed position, the Americans sent back to Hollywood, and the errant son reminded that his mother knows him through and through. The class structure is rocked in *Relative Values* but not overturned, and it is indicative of Coward's social conservatism — his fundamental disbelief in social equality — that it should be so. What is surprising in the play is that Felicity's manner succeeds not just because it mows down all other effects,

like the manner of the Blisses in *Hay Fever* and of Elyot
and Amanda in *Private Lives*, but because it is morally
and socially sensitive. Always attuned to the changing
sensibility of his audience, Coward possibly thought it
tactful in 1951 to introduce a measure of social morality
into the traditionally amoral comedy of manners, particularly since he himself identified increasingly with the
peerage and obviously looked to the day when he would
become Sir Noel. *Relative Values* promises that Coward's
adopted class would endure in an age of relative values,
not just because its manners were droll, but because its
mores were moral.

3

The Light Comedies

Although the comedy of manners enjoys a special distinction in Coward's oeuvre, the majority of his works align themselves with other genres and traditions of the comic stage. The Comedy of Humors, as written by Ben Jonson, the Comedy of Intrigue, best exemplified by the plays of Mrs. Aphra Behn, and the Sentimental Comedy, as written by Sir Richard Steele and others who tempered the licentiousness of Restoration drama — all have a discernible influence upon Coward's comic technique.[1]

The most obvious influence upon Coward's sense of comedy, however, was the Edwardian music hall, with its elaborately inflected innocence, its tolerant, rib-poking humor, its archness, its overblown stylistics, its reluctance to clutter language with ideas. In many ways, music halls served Coward as a conduit of the older comic traditions. The inflexible Garry Essendine in *Present Laughter* has his prototype not only in the humor-ridden characters of Ben Jonson but in performers like Marie Lloyd and Little Tich, who delighted music-hall patrons by varying their routines while remaining obdurately themselves. Madame Arcati of barbaric dress and fey manner in *Blithe Spirit* is in some ways a throwback to the beloved Kate Carney, resplendent in "'Arriet's feathers"; and Cherry-May Waterton in *Nude with Violin* is the gay, raffish, and carefree hussy of countless music-hall sketches. The discreetly indiscreet women of *Fallen Angels* and *Quadrille* may have their origin in sentimental comedies of the eighteenth century, but for Coward they had more immediate origin in the many music-hall sketches and songs about women who discover, to morality's consternation, that the flesh must have its hour.

Because they substitute linguistic pratfalls for physical pratfalls and effete ideology for clownish behavior, Coward's light comedies must be classified as high comedy rather than as burlesque, but they are deeply informed by the hours young Coward spent watching the masters of low comedy perform in music halls. More than anything else, perhaps, Coward took from music-hall sketches his characteristic mix of nonchalance and passion. The music-hall comediennes who affected not to notice impudent "costers" stand behind the comic nonchalance of Ruth Condomine in *Blithe Spirit*, of the drunken wives in *Fallen Angels*, and of the Marchioness of Herendon in *Quadrille*, just as the eccentric maid and the aloof butler of burlesque stand behind Coward's stage servants.

This is not to say that Coward's light comedies are reducible to the music-hall sketch; it is to suggest, rather, that Cowardly sophistication was born in the music hall and never lost the impress of its style. *Fallen Angels*, *Present Laughter*, and *Blithe Spirit* are the best of Coward's light comedies, and they illumine his fidelity for over twenty-five years to the music-hall ideal of weightless good fun. Two of Coward's last plays, *Quadrille* and *Nude with Violin*, suggest the twilight of that ideal and an acknowledgment on the author's part that comedic fashion had passed him by.

Fallen Angels

Written in 1923, *Fallen Angels* is one of Coward's earliest plays and spent months going the round of West End managements until the success of *The Vortex* rendered any Coward play commercially viable. Anthony Prinsep produced the play in 1925 as a vehicle for the actress Margaret Bannerman, but Bannerman was compelled to leave the cast just four days before the opening when she suffered a nervous breakdown. To Coward's relief, Tallulah Bankhead plunged in and saved the production:

Her vitality has always been remarkable, but on that occasion it was little short of fantastic. She took that exceedingly long part at a run. She tore off her hat, flipped her furs into a corner, kissed Edna [Best], Stanley [Bell], me and anyone else who happened to be within reach and, talking incessantly about *Rain*, which Maugham had just refused to allow her to play, she embarked on the first act. In two days she knew the whole part perfectly, and on the first night gave a brilliant and completely assured performance. It was a *tour de force* of vitality, magnetism and spontaneous combustion.[2]

Bankhead's only concession to the circumstances of her performance was to look out a window during the course of the play and in her breathy, intense manner, exclaim "*Rain!*" The topical interpolation delighted everyone except Coward, who was a stickler for straight performances.

 Fallen Angels ran for several months on the strength both of Bankhead's following and of reviews that denounced it as immoral and a threat to the public weal. A favorite of repertory companies and theater groups, it has often been revived, but seldom with the straight performances the author wanted. Hermione Gingold and Hermione Baddeley infuriated Coward when they accommodated the play to their stage personalities in a 1949 revival, but he eventually became reconciled to leading ladies commandeering the script. When a septuagenarian Gingold sought the rights for a South African revival many years after her first revival of the play, Coward gave reluctant approval but was heard to mutter that the age of sixty should really be the limit for playing his young heroines.[3]

In the first act of *Fallen Angels*, the good friends Julia Sterroll and Jane Banbury confide to each other that they have received postcards announcing the imminent arrival of Maurice Duclos, a Frenchman with whom they were intimate, seriatim, before meeting their husbands. Each woman has a presentiment that his arrival will disturb her comfortably unromantic marriage, and after their husbands Frederick and William depart for a weekend of golfing, they decide to run away to avoid an encounter they know will be indiscreet. The ringing of the doorbell stops their flight, and with one accord they drop their suitcases, prepared to accept Duclos as their fate. Actually, it is a plumber.

In the second act, the two women are elaborately gowned and waiting for Duclos's arrival, apparently having dropped their good resolves as permanently as their suitcases. As the hours drag on, they help themselves liberally to cocktails and then a bottle of champagne, and jealousy and mistrust well up between them. Julia orders Jane to leave her apartment, and Jane announces she will go straight to Duclos, with whom she claims to be in secret contact.

Act III takes place the following morning. Having quarreled with Frederick, William Banbury shows up unexpectedly at the Sterroll flat to reclaim his wife, only to have downcast Julia announce that Jane has left him for Duclos. They leave in search of Jane, and Frederick returns almost immediately, as does Julia, who has spent the night alone in a hotel. They discover a telephone message from Duclos left by the maid, and they erroneously conclude the worst — that Julia has run off with Duclos. This is disproven when Julia and William return, but the two men are infuriated that their wives never told them about Duclos. At that point Duclos enters, oozing Gallic charm. Quickly grasping the situation, he assures the husbands that it has all been a hoax to make them feel a stronger sense of sexual responsibility toward their wives. As the husbands digest that improvisation, Duclos and the two women retire to his flat just upstairs, and we hear them sing a song from which the play takes its name, "*Même les anges succombent à l'amour.*" "*Je t'aime,*" Duclos sings with feeling, and the curtain comes down as the husbands look at one another with stricken faces.

Fallen Angels is among the most thinly plotted of Coward's plays. In some ways it seems unfinished: the quarrel between William and Frederick is comedically undeveloped as a parallel to the women's quarrel, and Coward promises more in his anticipation of the plumber's entrance than he delivers. We expect a maid named Jasmin to score wittily in retaliation for Julia's renaming her Saunders on the theory that her given name is too "sticky" for the house, but Coward uses the maid only to move props about the stage and to interrupt conversations. Our expectation of richer plot development is an inevitable legacy of the well-made play, in which every aspect of the situation and every prop must have its dramatic outcome.

But Coward was less interested in writing a well-made play in 1923 than in orchestrating dialogue, and it is the cross talk of articulate characters that develops the play's conflict between psychological sophistication and the carnal itch. In an archly splendid mix of conceits, Julia observes that she and Jane have thrown their bonnets over a windmill, and with offhandedness equally arch, Jane sees their husbands as different from Duclos — nicer, and worthier, but not half as shattering to the soul. From behind a newspaper, Julia announces that a woman named Muriel Fenchurch is divorcing her husband, and Frederick answers dryly that the divorce is notably generous of the man. When Jane tries to put Duclos off by writing him a note in schoolgirl French to the effect that she and Julia are happily married, Julia proposes she add "Isn't it fun?" as if marriage were no less a sport than infidelity.

Psychological awareness adds comedic depth to such

dialogue. Having read their Freud, Coward's flappers view themselves dispassionately, almost as if they were psychoanalytic case studies. Part of what they dispassionately view is their own libidinal eruptions—about which they are fatalistic. The net effect is a dispassionate commitment to passion, a considered indulgence of the carnal instinct. Both women have analyzed their marriages and concluded that they love their husbands without being to any degree *in* love with them. As prelude to summing up their situation with healthy, modern objectivity, Julia proposes they lay out their situation like a card game and evaluate their hands. In doing so, they are quickly forced to the realization that they are completely happy except for an absence of violent emotion in their lives. The beast in them that sprang at Duclos once before is ready to spring again, they deduce, and Julia concludes her diagnosis with the excessively forthright observation that they are ripe for an indiscretion.

The women's ability to see their situation in psychological terms plays nicely against their awareness of a beast within waiting to spring, their awareness, too, of atavistic presentiments and unlucky coincidences. Julia and Jane are aggressively modern women who can entertain the notion of having an affair without seriously flinching, but beneath the veneer of their sophistication lie jealousy, lust, and a cavalier impulse to indulge their baser instincts. When Julia insists fervidly that the same windmill over which they threw their respective bonnets is coming to wreck them, Jane wails childishly that she doesn't want to be wrecked. Having induced this elemental wail, Julia restores cosmopolitan dignity with the voice of upstairs decorum and shushes her lest Saunders be scandalized.

Coward was right to be indignant with actresses who ignored this tension between sophistication and gaucherie when they accommodated the play to their individual talents. When the two women pledge to resume friendship and intimacy after the jealousy they know will develop when Ducloss makes his choice between them, the scene depends partially for its effect upon their educated ear for clichés, and partially upon their prejudging themselves (however thrilledly) of indecorum, but it depends ultimately on the counterpoint of this sophistication with the atavistic jealousies that they foresee.

The second act is the strongest in the play because the pit of vulgarity looms blacker as the two women become progressively drunk. Realizing that Duclos is long overdue, Jane worries that the effects they have arranged for him are ruined. Their idea was for Duclos to arrive unexpectedly and discover them quietly dining together in domestic surroundings, she says, not twiddling their thumbs and looking eager in a room decorated like a Bridal Suite. Julia objects to Jane's image of the Bridal Suite as vulgar and tries to raise the tone by offering a salted almond — which she unaccountably *throws* to Jane, who has to root for it in the sofa.

Such setbacks in behavior are only momentary, but they puncture the women's sophistication relentlessly. Jane asks why Julia was glad to find the plumber at the door when they had expected Duclos, and Julia is so guarded in her reply that the audience imagines toilet facilities steeped in iniquity. Feeling the effect of their cocktails, they begin to rhapsodize libidinously about Duclos's physical charms — his hands, teeth, *legs* — but when Saunders enters they switch abruptly into platitudes they imagine to be discreet. Julia complains witlessly that the cushions of carriages are always so dusty, to which Jane responds nervously that a nameless "she" ought never to have been burned at the stake, as she was basically a nice girl. It is Coward's joke that his psychologically sophisticated flappers are too inebriated to realize that their non sequiturs hint at a recumbent experience of carriages and at punishment fantasies all too appropriate. Under the influence of their drinking, a bathetic death wish for their husbands even wells up from the women's subconscious minds, and they weave a course from fantasy to guilt to repression to fantasy again, word by associational word. A taste for melodrama is among the several vulgar appetites that lurk beneath the women's sophistication.

In Act III the women abandon themselves whole-heartedly to the vulgarity emergent in Act II and show themselves both wrathful and rude. The elegant Julia becomes a bad-tempered harridan, snarling at Saunders over the distinction between a soft-boiled egg and an *un*-boiled egg, and she goes on to complain of a long dark hair in the marmalade. A hapless telephone operator who tells her Jane's line is engaged is called both incompetent and stupid. When William arrives, he is accused of tiresomeness, pigheadedness, and ninnyhood. In response to dark innuendos about Jane, William requests that Julia remember she is referring to his wife, and she crudely retorts that he is an optimist. Jane is almost as irascible. She snaps at Frederick that what she does is no business of his, and when he insists on knowing what has happened, she refuses on principle to discuss her former friend — except to say that Julia is hypocritical, treacherous, and completely immoral.

Despite this lapse into bad manners, the stylized syntax and clash of dictional modes continue to impart an arch flavor to the dialogue. Julia says to William that it would be well to stop abusing her and go in search of his wife, who, if she hasn't found Maurice Duclos, is probably wandering the streets in "deep" evening dress and hiccuping. "Deep" is a nice touch of wit, with its evocation of "deep mourning." William suggests that she can't have gone far, and Julia retorts that she has probably "gone" farther than "our" wildest dreams. Her tone is crudely sarcastic, but the word play on "gone" and the precise use of "our" are adroit.

The final scene of the play is as cavalier as the plot is thin. Duclos's taking all in hand and maneuvering the women to his flat is an improbable development but suited to the light-heartedness of the play—a gaily amoral climax to the libido's overthrow of psychological sophistication, and a fitting put-down of husbands less emotionally aware than their wives. One suspects it was no more than a whimsy on Coward's part to resolve the play in such fashion, for the situation might have been resolved equally well by a telegram canceling Duclos's visit. Yet it is a measure of *Fallen Angel*'s stature as light comedy that the ending is without resonance. The play's charm is the holiday it offers from Freudian hermeneutics and moral righteousness, the valuation it affords of lives animated by cleverness and wit.

Present Laughter

Present Laughter was written in 1939, under the shadow of a coming World War, and Coward confessed in his autobiography that he did not expect it ever to be produced.[4] To his surprise, the play managed to reach dress rehearsal on August 30, 1939, but plans for its opening were suspended when war broke out in the first days of September. Finally brought to the stage in 1942, *Present Laughter* continued to grieve its author. A tour of provincial cities prior to the London opening promised success, but a run at the Haymarket Theatre in London survived for only thirty-eight performances. A successful 1947 revival ran for eighteen months, but a simultaneous American production seemed to Coward "a gruesome evening." The production was "lamentable," he opined; Clifton Webb in the lead role was "lacking in fire and virility," and the supporting cast was "tatty and fifth rate."[5] An ill-advised French production in 1948 was very nearly a debacle; Hollywood interest in the play died aborning; and efforts to bring the play to American television in 1956 were stymied.

It was particularly irritating to Coward that Clifton

Webb's playing of the lead role in *Present Laughter* was cemented in the public mind as an auctorial portrait. There was a great deal of self-portraiture in the character, certainly, but in playing the Coward persona as a waspish tyrant, Webb was unfaithful not only to the script but also to Coward's own performances in the role.[6] Inexplicably, Webb's interpretation still dominates more gentle interpretations of the play and still serves to caricature the author.[7]

Set entirely in the London studio of Garry Essendine, a successful actor, the play begins early in the morning with pajama-clad Daphne Stillington making embarrassed excuses for her presence to Garry's employees: a housekeeper, Miss Erikson; a valet, Fred; and a secretary, Monica Reed. The staff are accustomed to such overnight guests and barely remark her presence. They are equally unflappable when their employer emerges from his bedroom, histrionically angry to have been awakened and disconcerted to find Daphne still in residence. Garry would like Daphne to decamp immediately, but his actor's instinct to charm leaves her believing she is the love of his life—until she is introduced to Liz Essendine, his estranged but still attentive wife. The morning takes its cue increasingly from French farce. Garry is unnerved when Roland Maule, a psychotic young playwright he has befriended, turns nasty; and Liz frets that Joanna Lyppiatt, the wife of playwright Hugo Lyppiatt, will make trouble for them all by her vamping of Morris Dixon, Garry's producer. The general turmoil is compounded by the news that Garry's leading lady has broken her leg and will be unable to accompany him on a repertory tour of African cities.

Act II takes place three days later and begins shortly after midnight. As Garry is preparing to retire, Joanna arrives at his door, intent suddenly upon seducing the great actor. The next morning she emerges from the spare bedroom, wearing the same dishabille as Daphne and offering the same, half-thought excuses for her presence to the household staff. Confusion develops even more quickly than in Act I, for Joanna's indiscretion threatens to tear apart the web of personal and professional relationships that binds Garry's entourage together. The confusion escalates: Morris Dixon and Hugo Lyppiatt come looking for Joanna with fire in their eyes; Roland Maule forces his way into the studio again; and a titled patroness brings her niece — Daphne Stillington — to audition for the role of Garry's leading lady.

Act III takes place on the last evening before Garry must depart for Africa. Preparing once again to retire, he is suddenly interrupted by Daphne, who is determined to accompany him to Africa as his mistress if she cannot accompany him as his leading lady. Roland Maule also makes a late-night entrance, and when Garry threatens to have the crazed young man thrown out by the police, Maule locks himself in the study. Joanna is another late-night caller, also determined to accompany Garry to Africa. In a panic, their unwilling host summons Liz, who becomes still another entrant into the African entourage and nominates herself to keep the other women in line. When Hugo and Morris arrive, mutually indignant that Joanna intends to run away with Garry, the great actor explodes. Morris has been carrying on an affair with Joanna, he informs Hugo, and he tells Joanna that the cuckolded Hugo has maintained a mistress for several months. This orgy of truth-telling drives everyone from the room except Liz, who announces blithely that she is coming back to Garry for good. Garry whispers to her that the situation is the reverse — that he is coming back to her — and they tiptoe from the studio to evade the mad playwright still locked in the study.

There is no question that *Present Laughter* was forged from elements in Coward's life. Those who dealt with him socially or professionally were quick to realize that Monica Reed was based on Lorn Loraine, his beloved secretary-manager; that Miss Erikson was the housekeeper he employed at his Belgravia flat; and that Garry Essendine, with his dressing gowns, histrionics, and entourage, was The Master himself. Even Coward's critics are represented in the play—specifically in Roland Maule, whose denunciation of Garry as a superficial, frivolous, and merely witty playwright is almost a transcription of the charges Coward had to endure regularly from the Beaverbrook press.[8]

But Coward was not simply indulging an autobiographical impulse in *Present Laughter*. Too much of a professional for such a self-serving enterprise, he was writing about what he knew best and what was always his best comic subject—the theatrical temperament. Garry Essendine is irrepressibly theatrical, the sort of person who cannot resist a dramatically effective line no matter what its affront to good sense. He gravely doubts that he shall ever be able to sleep again, he tells Liz, more histrionically than believably. "Here's your sordid little comb," he says to Monica with infamous adjectival abandon. When Fred announces that Lady Saltburn is at the door and claims to have an appointment, Monica gives a secretarial cry of surprise and asks the day. Garry cannot repress the sepulchral, dramatically overripe, "Black Thursday." As he prepares for his African tour, he wonders plaintively if he will ever see England again, and when Monica seems untouched, he suggests that he might die of some awful tropical disease or be bitten by a snake. Monica responds that there are probably not *many* snakes in the *larger* cities, but Garry is not ready to abandon the plaintive note and imagines himself under a mosquito net, fighting for breath. "Who with?" Monica queries, unmoved.

As Monica's query suggests, Garry is surrounded by initiates in the theater who are immune to histrionic flourish. Fred refers to the great man irreverently as "His Nibs"; Liz, as "God." Preparing to leave for the evening,

Miss Erikson asks if Garry has everything he wants, and
he answers he has not — has *anyone* what he wants? Immediately she is relieved, realizing that he is only acting.
When Joanna tries to seduce him, Garry pulls out all
theatrical stops and tells her that underneath his glittering veneer he is fundamentally honest. He can see through
her when he is driven into a corner, he says; he knows
what she is after and can see through every trick. "Curtain!" cries Joanna, laughing.

Yet Garry tells many truths despite such general
mockery: that he *is* kind and finds it difficult to put people off; that he *is* irritated beyond measure by those who
take his actor's charm too seriously; that he *is* fundamentally honest. The critic John Lahr has argued that
Garry is "a man who dissimulates so eagerly that he has
forgotten who he is,"[9] but in actuality Garry seems to
know full well his tendency to treat the world as a stage.
Daphne insists fervidly that he wasn't acting when he
made love to her, but Garry insists with equal fervidness
that he is always acting. Indeed, he brings to his insistence a self-evidencing touch of theatrical bravura and
agonizes that he is always acting, always watching himself go by, and that that is what is so horrible. He is never
incensed at being told he is acting a part, only at the
charge he *over*acts. He readily accepts himself as an actor, in contradistinction to some of the other characters,
who are loath to recognize their self-deceptions and public deceits. It is he who cries at the play's climax that the
others should stop being theatrical, and it is he in the
denouement who drives Joanna, Hugo, and Morris from
the studio, their performances collapsed and their deceits
exposed.

The parallelism of the several scene- and act-begin-
nings in the play reinforces this impingement of theatricality on the life of the characters. Daphne's emergence
from the spare bedroom at the beginning of Act I is par-
alleled exactly by Joanna's emergence in the second scene

of Act II, and Joanna's late-night intrusion at the beginning of Act II is echoed in Daphne's entrance, suitcase in hand, at the beginning of Act III. In an ironic echo of the first of these parallels, Liz pops out of the spare bedroom just when Hugo and Morris are convinced that Joanna is hiding in the room; and in an ironic echo of the second parallel, Garry decides to resume cohabitation with Liz. Roland Maule's intrusive entrances reverberate from act to act in a similar manner. Indeed, the profusion of intrusive entrances in the play comes to seem a theatrical convention run amok, for such an extreme stylization of happenstance evokes the arrangements of art rather than of life.

Dramaturgically, this profusion of similar entrances suggests two important meanings: that life offers a limited number of scenes, and that the actor who hopes to be proficient in life must recognize his cues. Monica is adept at such cues, as when she asks Daphne in Act I if Garry mentioned the previous evening that Life was passing him by. When Daphne admits that he mentioned something like that, Monica is immediately dismayed, knowing that Garry has given a full performance. Liz is as well schooled as Monica in her cues, knowing that her invariable gift of a dressing gown will infallibly please a man besotted with dressing gowns and knowing that it is her role to save Garry from those he has charmed. As adept as Garry at creating scenes but more cynical than he in arranging them, the two women discuss whether they must stage a *big* scene, "a real rouser," to stop him from complicating his love life further. Only Garry, the professional actor, tries continually to break off scenes he cannot play, however often they are repeated. Only Garry cannot learn his cues — because, ironically, he brings to every scene an actor's excruciating sincerity.

This focus on the theatrical temperament and its pitfalls imparts a special vibrancy to the dialogical exchanges in *Present Laughter*. The usual cut-and-thrust of domestic affections in a Coward play becomes in *Present Laughter* a battle of the theatrical boards, richly hyperbolic and professionally ruthless. When Monica reminds Garry that he has an imminent appointment with Roland Maule, Garry asks disingenuously who Maule is, and with a rhetorical overkill born of theatrical privity, Monica immediately quashes all possibility of his breaking the appointment. She tells him that he knows perfectly well, that Maule is the young man who wrote a mad play half in verse and caught him on the telephone, and that Garry was so busy being attractive and unspoiled by his success that he promised him an appointment. Skilled himself at such rhetorical overkill, Garry counters as fulsomely that he has noticed a great change in Monica lately— a change in personality due possibly to her cramming herself with potatoes. The exchange is quite innocent of bad feeling; such stylized, theatrical invective is simply Garry's and Monica's way of striking a balance. Even Love has to upstage other performances to gain a hearing, and Liz finds it necessary to upstage Garry cruelly in order to express her genuine concern for his wellbeing.

Present Laughter's focus on the theatrical temperament lends a special vibrancy not only to the success of its dialogue but to the failures of its dialogue as well. Coward had a fine ear for the overexplanations of guilt, but in *Present Laughter* such explanations are not only droll but, more interestingly, a failure of performance. Pajamaed Daphne chirps nervously to the staff that Mr. Essendine drove her home the previous night from a party, and she idiotically forgot her latchkey, and so he sweetly said she could stay with him — in the spare room, she adds limply. The non sequitur born of frenzy was also one of Coward's strengths but never more perfectly pitched than when it was also a failure in dramatic improvisation. Garry has to dissuade Morris from going to

Liz's flat in search of Joanna, and so he announces that
Morris is coming with him. Innocently, Morris enquires
where they are going. "Westminster Abbey" is Garry's
rattled, wonderfully random reply.

   Present Laughter is one of Coward's most successful
plays because it is a continual stream of such effortlessly
comic moments. One must have a taste for French farce,
perhaps, to appreciate its whirligig dramatics, but only
a handful of Coward's plays — *Private Lives, Design for
Living, Blithe Spirit* — surpass it for hilarious inflection
and general playability. For the student of Coward's life,
Present Laughter has the additional charm of being The
Master's meditation on an actor's need to believe and yet
disbelieve in his own illusions. If the play suggests acer-
bically that the quicksilver adulation of fans endangers
the actor's sense of self, Coward's gratitude to his personal entourage for treating him with unillusioned indulgence lends the play a compensatory heart. Miraculous-
ly, that heart in no way sentimentalizes the play. *Present
Laughter* is that rarest of rarities — a work intensely personal in its interest and entirely professional in its craft.

Blithe Spirit

Unlikely as it may seem at first glance, *Blithe Spirit* is
a play born of Coward's determination to serve his country in World War II. Rebuffed by the British War Office
when he volunteered his services and dismissed by Win-
ston Churchill with a suggestion that he spend the war
singing "Mad Dogs and Englishmen" for the troops,
Coward decided his substantial contribution to the war
effort had to be as a writer. Patriotism was his theme in
the film *In Which We Serve* (1942) and in the songs
"London Pride" and "There Will Be Songs in England,"
but lightness seemed to him just as important a note to
sound as love of country, and he tried to jolly his coun-

trymen with songs like "Don't Let's Be Beastly to the Germans" and "Could You Please Oblige Us with a Bren Gun." *Blithe Spirit* (1941) was his most lissome gift to a nation spiritually fatigued and patriotically overtaxed. Evidencing the nation's hunger for such comedy, audiences packed London performances of the play for a record-setting four and one-half years (1997 performances).[10] "I shall ever be grateful," Coward wrote years later, "for the almost psychic gift that enabled me to write *Blithe Spirit* in five days during one of the darkest years of the war."[11]

As *Blithe Spirit* begins, Ruth Condomine is trying to restrain a servant girl named Edith, who performs her household tasks with indecorous energy. Ruth is the second wife of Charles Condomine, a writer, and together they are awaiting their three dinner guests: Doctor and Mrs. Bradman, and Madame Arcati, a neighborhood medium. A séance is scheduled for after dinner, inasmuch as Charles is writing a novel about spiritualism and likes to take his scenes from life. Hoping Madame Arcati will be a fraud, he is disconcerted to find she is a hearty, as devoted to her bicycle and to dry martinis as to her ghostly control, who is an adenoidal and unstable child named Daphne. He is even more disconcerted when Madame Arcati's séance causes Elvira, his first wife, to materialize for his eyes and ears only. His problem is not only the psychical ménage à trois but Elvira's lethal talent for mischief. By the end of Act I, Ruth is indignant over rude remarks that Charles seems to be addressing to her but is really addressing to Elvira, and the irrepressible Elvira is congratulating herself on one of the most enjoyable half hours she has ever spent stirring up trouble.

Act II traces Ruth's slow realization that her husband is neither drunk nor insane but haunted. Madame Arcati is summoned to exorcise Elvira but has to confess that she does not know how, and she leaves in a professional

huff when Ruth accuses her of amateur muddling. Elvira, however, is delighted to learn of Madame Arcati's
exit and begins to booby-trap the house. The maid Edith
is concussed after slipping on a stair tread covered with
axle grease, and Charles fractures his wrist when a van-
dalized ladder collapses beneath him. Ruth is shrewd
enough to realize that Elvira is trying to kill Charles so
that he will have to join her in eternity, and she takes
Charles's car — also sabotaged by Elvira — in a mad rush
to consult Madame Arcati. The act ends with Charles
receiving a telephone message that Ruth has been killed
in an automobile crash. Simultaneously, an invisible presence buffets Elvira, and she cries out to Ruth to desist.

Act III takes place several days later. Realizing that
Elvira has sent Ruth to her death, Madame Arcati attempts to dematerialize Elvira, but only succeeds in ma-
terializing Ruth, and the two wives become increasingly
petulant at being subjected to Madame Arcati's efforts
to expunge them with what Ruth regards as unwar-
rantedly insulting verses. It has always been Madame
Arcati's contention that someone in the house called the
wives back from the spirit world, and Charles has always
insisted it was not he. With the aid of her crystal ball and
a magical incantation, Madame Arcati suddenly exposes
the maid Edith as the natural medium who is responsible, and after casting Edith into a trance, she is apparently successful in getting her to dispatch the ghosts. It
is Coward's last joke, however, that the two wives simply
dematerialize. As the final curtain descends, Charles
taunts the vanished women with his escape from their
clutches, and they revenge themselves with an outbreak
of poltergeist violence.

As the critic John Lahr has suggested, *Blithe Spirit*
can be understood as a working out of "survivor guilt."[12]
Only a month before the play was written, the Luft-
waffe had bombed Coward's Gerald Road flat while he
was out to dinner, and three nights later, newly ensconced

at the Savoy, he watched walls bulge and a door blow in as bombs fell outside the famous hotel. Death took its toll all around him, but The Master survived. His diary for 1941 talks of walking around devastated London — "The whole city a pitiful sight"[13] — and he notes wryly that the English did not take their pleasures unwillingly in the midst of death and destruction. Like the people of Plymouth whom he saw dancing on the Hoe and like the audiences who flocked to see *Blithe Spirit*, Coward must have experienced an atavistic need to banish the dead from consciousness. More than that, he must have suffered subconscious guilt at the wish to get on with life. As a play that banishes ghosts, *Blithe Spirit* should probably be understood as an exorcism of such guilt.

But one can overemphasize the wartime psychology of the play. *Blithe Spirit* is timelessly appreciable as an exercise in comic incongruity, with its focus an off-balancing, too-easy relationship between the ordinary and the occult. Coward's ghosts are not bed-sheeted spooks but elegant gray ladies who retain in death the bitchy vitality they possessed in life. They are not so much symbolic eruptions of guilt or repressed sexuality as inconvenient presences unwillingly summoned and uncomfortably ensconced in what Ruth considers a mortifying position — not quite fish, flesh, or fowl. Very little more than they were in life, they retain all their mortal faults. Charles remarks to Elvira that seven years' residence in the choir invisible has in no way diminished her native vulgarity, and she is indeed the charming vulgarian he remembers, given to the off-color remark, the rude challenge, the mortifying reminiscence. Correspondingly, Ruth continues in death as the ruthlessly efficient matron who thinks careless rapture incongruous and embarrassing in a second marriage.

Madame Arcati is the only character in the play at ease with this too-easy domestication of the dead, probably because she herself exists with one foot in her En-

glish garden and one foot in eternity. Her ingenous approach to the unknown is a reproach to spiritualistic
hocus-pocus on the one hand, a challenge to intellectual
disbelief on the other. She is so completely at home with
the spiritual world that she mentions her conversations
with the dead as if they were the stuff of ordinary gossip,
yet she makes it artlessly clear that she is no clairvoyant
and that she disapproves of fortune tellers. She worries
in a practical way if someone will trip over her bicycle
in the dark only a moment after listening to birdsong at
an open window and observing madly, psychically,
"That cuckoo is very angry." Her speech is replete with
girl-guide slogans even when she is discussing the supernatural. "Heigho, heigho, to work we go!" she intones
in an endearing echo of Walt Disney's dwarfs as she organizes a séance, and she relentlessly enjoins Charles to
keep his "chin up," to force his "shoulder to the wheel,"
to put his "back really in it." Such clichés are funny not
only for their plebeian heartiness but because they ema-
nate so incongruously from a professional medium.

Madame Arcati is also a naïf, her status as the most
spiritually erudite mortal in the play notwithstanding.
She is thrilled when Elvira blows contemptuously in her
ear, and her fond references to that malign spirit as "the
darling" and "the dear" reflect a misunderstanding of
Elvira's character that borders on lunacy. Irony cannot
touch her self-containment. Annoyed that the Madame
is proud of having materialized Elvira, Ruth comments
nastily, "From your own professional standpoint I can
see that it might be regarded as a major achievement!"
"A triumph, my dear!" Madame Arcati responds with
unalloyed pride in her professional view point. Only
a challenge to her seriousness of purpose penetrates Madame Arcati's benighted poise. When Ruth asks if she
realizes what her amateur muddling has done, Madame
Arcati draws herself up with the dignity of unflappable
self-assurance and points out that she has been a profes-

sional since she was a child—that "amateur" is a word she will not tolerate.

Such characterization is crucial to the success of *Blithe Spirit* as a play, for it lends a winsome charm to stage business and plot developments occasionally in danger of seeming facile. Elvira's bringing a bowl of flowers within an inch of unbelieving Ruth's nose is a necromantic scene so predictable in type that it would be tiresome without the character development that makes all of Elvira's actions seem the inspired naughtiness of a coquette. Ruth's pummeling of Elvira as the curtain descends on Act II would be vulgar slapstick had Ruth not been characterized as too ineffably high-minded in her own view to indulge such a mode of revenge. Similarly, Charles's spiteful remarks at the final curtain would seem claptrap had he not checked his tongue so deferentially and for so long a period while his wives' tongues ran amok.

This comically incongruous characterization is all the more comic for its psychological probity. Coward has seldom been credited with insight into the human soul, but he had a good sense of the ordinary dynamics of psychology and built his wittiest scenes from such durable factors of consciousness as jealousy, mean-spiritedness, and ennui. The three spouses of *Blithe Spirit* are entirely explicable as they rub against one another like sandpaper, shredding their silken sophistication to pieces, and the incongruous professionalism of Madame Arcati is equally explicable as it cuts across the grain of their decorum like a rasp. The unstable border between comic exaggeration and psychological wisdom is, indeed, the explosive edge of *Blithe Spirit*'s comedy. There is no finer moment in the play than that in which Madame Arcati is solicitous for the two wives' peace of mind while Ruth fears that if precautions are not taken, the Madame is apt to materialize a hockey team. Ruth's fantasy of the hockey team is provoked by her husband's show of re-

straint, which is really weariness with his wives' distem-
per, and the sexually libidinous overtone of the fantasy—
unusual in Ruth—is comically credible precisely because
Charles is showing weakness. At the same time, Madame
Arcati's question is perfectly pitched to suggest her professional detachment as compromised by an understandable fondness for the spooks she has materialized and by
her willingness to prolong the hour of astral triumph.
The three points of view are played in concert, and the
net effect is a richly textured moment of drama, its psychological soundness a factor of its comic efferves-
cence.

Psychological and comedic understandings combine
nicely when Ruth decides that Charles is hallucinating
and wants him to go to bed so that she can summon Dr.
Bradman to treat him. As Ruth reassures Charles that
she understands everything and pats his arm reassuring-
ly, Elvira warns him in a voice Ruth cannot hear that
she is up to something and comments that her wanting
Charles to go to bed is blatantly erotic. *She* had no trouble getting him into bed at midmorning, she recalls sala-
ciously, and Charles snaps at her with an impatience
Ruth has to think directed at herself, but in response to
which she cannot afford to take offense. The three states
of mind are utterly at odds. Ruth is aggressively understanding; Charles, badly rattled; Elvira, carnal-minded
as always—and the result is confusion of a high comedic
order.

Coward orchestrates such scenes in many different
keys. Ruth shows herself reluctant to continue an argument in the presence of the servants, and Charles is
stimulated by their presence to argue more strenuously
than before. The result is a marital counterpoint that
defines the husband's and wife's different relationships
to the servants and the different modes of their ner-
vousness. As Madame Arcati organizes her séance, she
worries Ruth by mentioning that a poltergeist would be

extremely destructive, discomforts Mrs. Bradman with the observation that an Elemental would probably take the form of a very cold wind, and stupefies Dr. Bradman with an injunction to empty his mind. Then, in passing a mirror, she stops and adjusts her hair — a primping for her ghostly guests that is endearing in the context of her alarms and comically unexpected in a woman we had thought unconscious of her appearance. In another scene, perhaps the most economically crafted in the play, Charles presses a pound note into Edith's hand and murmurs a thank-you after she appears to have dispatched the ghosts successfully. With no recollection of having done anything to warrant this largesse, Edith asks what the gratuity is for. Then, countless stories of masters and unconscious maids apparently welling up in her mind, she looks at him in sudden horror, cries, "Oh sir!!" and bolts from the room.

All these scenes are largely innocent of satire. *Blithe Spirit* is a drawing room comedy of the most rarefied type in that it is psychologically astute but moralistically featherweight, in that it violates taboos with impunity but carefully avoids social criticism. Coward has several times been linked to the dramatists William Congreve and Richard Brinsley Sheridan,[14] who brought drawing room comedy to a momentary perfection, but *Blithe Spirit* distinguishes Coward from those predecessors as sometimes a more "polite" dramatist. It may be true, as the American critic George Jean Nathan once observed, that "polite comedy . . . is polite only as a servant is polite, that is, for business reasons,"[15] but in *Blithe Spirit* Coward proved that psychological, nonsatirical humor can create drawing room comedy of rare distinction. That *Blithe Spirit* was commercially one of his most successful plays (and enjoyed a second success as the basis for Hugh Martin and Thomas Gray's musical play *High Spirits*) is evidence less of Coward's eye to the box office than of his theatrical acumen.

Quadrille

While visiting with Alfred Lunt and Lynn Fontanne at their Wisconsin home in 1951, Coward promised to write another play for the theatrical couple, his first for them since *Design for Living* in 1933 and *Point Valaine* in 1934. It would be a romantic Victorian comedy, they agreed, and early in 1952 the Lunts were delighted when Coward presented them with the completed script of *Quadrille*. Rehearsals and a tour of provincial cities during the summer of 1952 went well, but the London opening in September was darkened by the death barely a week before of Coward's long-time friend, the actress Gertrude Lawrence. His sense of loss was profound: the very theater in which *Quadrille* opened echoed with memories of Lawrence's performances in *Private Lives* and *Tonight at 8:30*, and both the popular success and the critical failure of *Quadrille* seemed negligible to Coward in the context of his friend's death. Lynn Fontanne was understandably hurt to read in *The Times* what Coward had said of Lawrence: "No one I have ever known, however brilliant and however gifted, has contributed quite what she contributed to my work."[16]

Quadrille opens in the Buffet de la Gare, Boulogne, in the year 1873. Hubert, the Marquis of Heronden, and Charlotte Diensen, the wife of an American railroad magnate, are running away together to Nice, hoping their respective spouses will agree to divorce them. An oleaginous clergyman, the Reverend Spevin, is also en route to Nice, and he strikes up a conversation with the marquis and his apparent consort in hopes of their patronage. Hubert is preoccupied with Charlotte's fear that his wife Serena will not divorce him, and he puts off the clergyman with the promise of a subscription. The scene then shifts to Serena's sitting room overlooking Belgrave Square. In the company of a friend, Lady Harriet Ripley, Serena is handed Hubert's farewell note by her butler, and she struggles to retain the composure and dignity that are important to her. The arrival of Axel Diensen, Charlotte's husband, puts her composure to the test, but she agrees to join him in a pursuit of their errant spouses.

Act II takes place two days later at the Villa Zodiaque in Nice. Charlotte's worst fears are realized when Serena and Axel burst in upon the runaways at breakfast, Serena high-handedly, Axel ready for a scene of violence that is forestalled only by the Reverend Spevin who comes tapping at the window. By the next morning, both Serena and Axel are beginning to admire each other and wondering if they really want to reclaim their spouses, but Hubert and Charlotte quarrel and agree to separate, leaving Serena and Axel uneasy with their victory. As they prepare that evening to leave the Villa Zodiaque, Axel and Serena talk long and intimately, and Axel kisses the marchioness's hand.

A year passes before the advent of Act III, and the situation reverses itself in the interval. Serena is preparing to leave the Belgrave Square house, ostensibly for a vacation in the country, and Hubert announces a plan to go hunting with a Mr. Mallory in Africa. Lady Harriet discloses that Hubert has a new paramour — a Mrs. Mallory — but Serena's only comment is "poor Hubert." Serena is really on her way to join Axel at the Villa Zodiaque, we are certain, for without explaining her mood of gay excitement she gives Lady Harriet an heirloom brooch to remember her by and a letter to the butler to pass on to her husband. The last scene of the play mirrors the first: Axel and Serena take breakfast at the train station in Boulogne, and the Reverend Spevin interrupts once again, only slightly rattled by the shifting combinations of husband and wife. The play ends with the lovers walking onto the platform in a flood of sunshine, Axel assuring a worried Serena that their love has world enough and time.

Quadrille demands comparison with *Private Lives*.

Its insistent symmetries — the reciprocal infidelities, the eruption of the Reverend Spevin approximately midway in each act, the balanced machinery of exits and entrances — all recall the symmetries of *Private Lives*, although with important differences. The emotionally symmetric world of *Private Lives* is a force with which Elyot and Amanda must contend, whereas the symmetries of *Quadrille* are only a formal patterning, stately but inconsequential. It seems to us inevitable that Serena and Axel should elope at the end of Act III, turning the tables on their spouses, but glands and temperament have less to do with elopement, we sense, than quadrilateral neatness, and we cannot cheer their flight as we can Amanda and Elyot's. *Quadrille* has about it the formal balance of the dance formation for which it is named. In reviewing the New York première, Brooks Atkinson suggested appositely that it seemed less a play than a carefully measured dance.[17]

This static patterning in *Quadrille* enhances Coward's premise that the Victorians were lacking in vitality. Although Hubert has evidently a long history of philandering, Serena has to be told about both Charlotte and Mrs. Mallory, and though she says she loves her husband, she will confess to being concerned with his affairs only under the pressure of Axel's importunate questioning. Lady Harriet asks significantly how much Serena really minds when she refuses to show concern that Hubert has left her. Serena is not without passions: her views on the Albert Memorial amount to high treason, she tells us, and she brings down the curtain on Act I with a lusty "Hell and damnation!" Nevertheless, she has made a decision to behave admirably rather than to live deeply. She cherishes no romantic notions of winning her husband back, she says frostily; all she wants is to salvage a little dignity.

Although he has the courage to run away with

Charlotte, Hubert is only slightly more vital than the
serene Serena. His wife suggests his elopement is a sham,
that he fully intended she should give chase and reclaim
him. Charlotte also doubts Hubert's emotional vitality.
Is she really dear to him? she wonders. Has anyone ever
been dear to him? She accuses Hubert early in their
elopement of being light-headed, of living irresponsibly,
of "behaving like a bubble."

With their new-world vitality and directness, the
Americans Axel and Charlotte Diensen seem to offer a
contrast to the effete Marquis and Marchioness of Heronden. Axel commands the railways Hubert only dreams
of running, and he pursues his personal goals without
undue respect for the conventions of class or the appearance of dignity. He admires Serena when she refuses to
admit wifely chagrin that her husband has left her, but
he sees her upholding a chosen style of behavior, while
Serena thinks she is not "behaving" at all. As an Eliot
from Boston, Charlotte surpasses both the marquis and
marchioness in her respect for outraged propriety, but
as a steely-eyed American she prefers Boston to Arcadia
and will not be sidetracked by Hubert's fluency. Indeed,
she pleads with him to discuss their circumstances in simple terms. Whenever he sets out on a sentence, she remarks, she feels as though he were off on a long journey and that she should wave him goodbye. Although
devoted to conventions, she is too vital a person to love
so insubstantial a man as the marquis, and she finally
renounces him. She is willing to endure social ostra-
cism, she says, but not for one whose character is
"watery."

The effect of this difference in vitality between the
American and the British couples is undercut by a taste
they share for phrasemaking. Charlotte may object to
the marquis's rhetoric as overblown and to his character
as watery, but her tone in the speech alluded to above

makes clear that she is infected by the same taste for mannered speech as he. Are his words merely the flaking paint on old paneling? she enquires. As if she had challenged him to a duel, Hubert cannot resist capping her elaborate conceit, and he requests that she not suspect him of dry rot. Typically, the exchange is overwritten to the point of archness: its staginess belongs less to Coward's stage than to his characters' personalities, and its effect is to suggest a contest of manners in which each hopes to upstage the other.

Serena and Axel are capable of equally histrionic elaborations. Serena accuses Lady Harriet of bristling like a hedgehog and suggests that she would rent the butler if she brushed against him in the hall. Of her marriage, she says too fulsomely that she was malleable when the skies were clear and the breezes gentle, but that later, when winds of disillusion blew cold, her heart froze and her character suffered a sea change. Axel's speeches were greatly admired in the play's first productions,[18] especially his long speech in Act II about traversing the American continent, but we are surely meant to understand that speech as nineteenth-century grandiloquence, its effusions both Whitmanesque and stagy. Such mannered speeches are commonplace in *Quadrille*, and the challenging of one manner with another is the play's essential dynamic. The scene in which Axel and Serena plot their chase of the runaways is impossibly arch and ludicrously "thrilling," but it is also edged with Serena's awareness of Axel's exaggerations, and it is that kind of awareness that prevents such scenes from slipping into straightforward melodrama.

Serena's awareness of Axel's exaggeration also mocks the sort of drama that had become Coward's trademark. Stagy emotions and geometrically arrayed characters are staples of the Coward play but are seldom so archly artificial as in *Quadrille*. Almost textbook instances of overwriting, they lack the dramaturgical insouciance of

Coward's earlier plays but succeed as a parody of Victorian stylistics because of *Quadrille*'s period trappings. Indeed, a Victorian taste for exaggerated style both in morals and in drama is Coward's theme in the play, and the Victorian underpinnings of Coward's *own* theater — thought so brilliantly modern in the 1930s and so passé in the 1950s — is his joke. "Am I so entirely of the thirties?" he seems to ask. The whiff of old greasepaint and kerosene footlights in *Quadrille* avers a dramaturgy more passé than even Coward's detractors charged.

The Victorian stylistics of *Quadrille* are thrown into further relief by Octavia Bonnington, whose villa adjoins the Villa Zodiaque in Nice. An elderly countess who writes daringly improper books under the pseudonym Lucien Snow, she is a dithering old dear who bursts into Act II like a whirlwind and refuses to believe that Axel and Serena are not already lovers. She congratulates them rhapsodically for having turned their backs on outworn modesties and petty conventions, and pronounces them free to plunge laughing into mountain streams and to ride naked together in the meadows. She is the libertarian voice of café society in the 1930s turned aged and eccentric in the 1950s, yet she is the catalyst of Axel and Serena's eventual elopement. Coward is at once admitting the unfashionableness of his 1930 themes and proclaiming their relevance to a 1950s world still timidly Victorian at heart.

Quadrille has its longueurs, especially when the Reverend Spevin is on stage, but it is one of Coward's most gentle comedies, and its parody of Victorian stylistics is winning. It was Coward's genius to realize that *Private Lives* could not be updated for the Lunts in the 1950s, but that it might successfully be *out*dated — that the formula of his most acclaimed comedy of manners could be carried just a bit further, given period trappings, and be transformed from something temporarily out-of-date to something charmingly antique.

Nude with Violin

As Coward grew older and saw his reputation decline, he tended to complain about the regnant canons of taste. Formlessness was rampant in the arts, he argued, because critics were no longer sensitive to craftsmanship. That his own plays suffered increasingly from overwriting and from structures more plodding than inspired, he seemed not to realize. Rather, he saw the eclipse of his reputation as due entirely to the malevolence of reviewers who disdained his theatrics as old-fashioned and looked to "angry" dramatists like John Osborne as more in tune with the day. *Nude with Violin* (1956) was Coward's revenge. Portraying the art establishment as an unmitigated hoax, it pleased London audiences greatly for a time, but provoked reviewers. "There is obviously a quality in *Nude with Violin* which irritates the critical mind," Coward wrote contemptuously in his diary; "Perhaps because the whole play is a blistering satire on the critical mind?"[19]

Nude with Violin is set entirely in the Paris studio of Paul Sorodin, a recently deceased painter and an alleged giant of modernism. Gathered in the wake of his obsequies are Mme. Isobel Sorodin, his estranged wife; Jane and Colin, his adult children; Pamela, Colin's wife; Jacob Friedland, an art dealer who had handled all of Sorodin's affairs; and Sebastien Lecréole, the painter's polyglot valet. With the exception of Jane, the Sorodins mistrust Sebastien, even though he is elaborately deferential and does his best to hold at bay an enterprising journalist from *Life* magazine. Their mistrust is not lessened when Sebastien produces a letter from Sorodin which announces crowingly an elaborate hoax — that he had never painted any of the famous pictures bearing his signature.

Act II finds the unmourning mourners wondering how to avoid public disclosure of Sorodin's deception, especially in view of his studio containing one final paint-ing—the eponymous "Nude with Violin"—which might be sold for a great deal of money. Their efforts are brought up short by the arrival of the Princess Anya Pav-likov, who announces in a ravaged Russian accent that she had painted the pictures of Sorodin's "Farouche" period between 1925 and 1929, when Sorodin was her lover. Her purpose is blackmail, but through some in-explicable blackmail of his own, Sebastien is able to send her packing. Jane asks why her father perpetrated such a hoax, and Sebastien explains that it was an art lover's revenge upon dishonesty, cant, and the commercialism that had turned art into a business. His defense of Soro-din is cut short by the arrival of Cherry-May Waterton, a retired cockney chanteuse. She is the ghost painter of Sorodin's "Circular" period, she announces, and she has documentation to prove her claim. Before she can be dealt with, a Seventh Day Adventist arrives in the "very black" person of Mr. Obadiah Lewellyn. Sebastien real-izes immediately that he is the genius of the Jamaican period.

In Act III, Lewellyn has departed for Jamaica, having been persuaded to abandon his claim on Sorodin's reputation by some of Sebastien's friends in the under-world, and Cherry-May is satisfactorily bought off by Jacob. The last, "Neo-Infantilist," period of Sorodin's ca-reer remains a mystery until Sebastien's bastard son Lau-derdale bursts in, furious because his father has shown "Nude with Violin" before it was finished. Sorodin signed about thirty of young Lauderdale's canvases, Sebastien confesses, and he intends to sell the preposterously ama-teur works at collector's prices. Although angry, Jacob and Sorodins cannot forestall him, as they are already parties to the hoax. The play ends with art experts ar-riving to bid upon a painting known to them as "Rude with Violin."[20]

As several reviewers noted, *Nude with Violin* is

lacking in original wit. The art of modernist painters had
been the target of Philistine humor for at least two decades at the time the play was launched, and the notion
that one's child could paint as well as Picasso was a commonplace of the middlebrow viewpoint. No less commonplace was a conviction that the modernist painters
were charlatans, laughing all the way to the bank at
critics who had made them famous. These familiar jokes
had enough life in them to bear resuscitation, perhaps,
but what saved Coward's play from banality and helped
it to run successfully in London for a year was its lively
characterizations.

As he grew older, Coward was increasingly wont
to imagine his characters fully, regardless of how brief
their appearances on stage, and to fabricate for his own
satisfaction details of their lives without bearing upon
dialogue or plot. He liked to ask himself where the young
hero went to school, whether the ingenue had teased her
siblings, if the widowed butler had had a happy marriage. This compulsion to create rounded mental notions
of his characters was criticized by Cole Lesley and others, for it slowed the process of Coward's writing. A
more serious effect of the compulsion was a tendency for
Coward to blur his comic focus with characters more
complex than their function in the plot required.

Mme. Sorodin, for instance, is a minor character interestingly at odds with herself. A reserved Englishwom-
an made nervous by her French husband's reputation
for loose living, she feels a duty to conventional grief
although she has been separated from Sorodin for twen-
ty-nine years. She keeps a wary eye on the value of his
estate, although she is embarrassed by her son's franker
interest in its settlement, and she believes herself deeply
honest, though her daughter Jane's honesty throws her
limited honesty into comic relief. Slightly competitive integrity is her keynote. Assured that she is a woman of the
highest principles and a Catholic, the American jour-

nalist remarks casually, indifferently, "Can you beat that?" Sebastien's response — that people have tried without success — hints at unstaged scenes in the Sorodin marriage.

Jane is less completely sketched than her mother, but the honesty in her nature is complexly at odds with the flummery of the Sorodins, whether she is observing that her mother has had a most comfortable life or that her father's genius must be permitted to have found its scope. That Jane's opinion counts for little in the family and that she is never more than a small voice in the play make such remarks seem full of unreleased dramaturgical energy — an energy that might effectively shatter the smugness of her family and seize the third-act curtain for itself. Friedland and Colin contain similar energies that the plot does not release. Friedland tries desperately to keep the Sorodins focused on their public-relations problem as he envisions his career falling to pieces, and Colin is genuinely considerate of his mother, though insufferably venal and priggish. Neither man is the simple character for whom his role in the plot seems devised.

Cherry-May Waterton and the American journalist Clinton Preminger are more familiar Coward types, their whole characters unfurled on the surface of their roles. But with her inarticulate gigolo in tow, her sporting, live-and-let-live ethic, and her eye unabashedly on the main chance, Cherry-May is not only a foil for the genteel Sorodins but also their collective alter ego. She is Isobel's alter ego in her discovery that cohabitation with Sorodin is impossible; Pamela's, in her silliness about a young man; Colin's, in the frankness of her avarice; and Jane's, in her unerring sense of reality. Preminger is not only Coward's stage American — pushy, naïve, and incomprehensible in his idioms — but Friedland's alter ego, a parody of his need to organize, of his victimization by Sorodin, and of his art dealer's penchant for jargon. Together, Cherry-May and Preminger stir the waters of characterization into pools and eddies that distract from the simple flow of the plot. Ultimately, they help us to realize that Friedland and the Sorodins are not so much deluded by Paul Sorodin's hoax as by hoaxes they have perpetrated upon themselves.

Sebastien's dominant role in the play is undercut by this array of over-developed and cross-referencing minor characters. A former resident of prison cells in Johannesburg, Saigon, and the Belgian Congo, yet a man more embarrassed by a lack of taste than by any possible lack of funds, he is a deeply civilized criminal and an inherently comic character. Jane suggests that Sebastien is unscrupulous, and his response is typical: "Mademoiselle is too kind." But this man of paradoxical character spends much of the play eavesdropping offstage while Friedland and the Sorodins debate what is to be done, and his potentially fascinating arrangements with underworld lowlifes also transpire offstage. The result is a dramatic effacement not unsuited to his character but too deferential to the minor characters. The comic focus of the play suffers in consequence, for we find ourselves less interested in the hoax he has helped to perpetrate than in the more generally diffused ability of the characters to hoax themselves. In failing to come to a climax, that more general chicanery is not able to carry the plot.

A sloppiness about details also blurs the play's logic of design. Sebastien's blackmail of the Princess Anya Pavlikov is apparently based on the fact that she is currently married, but what bearing that fact has upon her claim to have ghosted the Farouche Period is not clear. Sorodin's detestation of critics is also inexplicable, inasmuch as he seems not to have been aesthetically sensitive, at least in terms of music. Sebastien develops a nice conceit when he observes that Sorodin could not distinguish between "Begin the Beguine" and "God Save the Queen." Apparently he continued all his life to rise for "Begin the Beguine."

"Well, Noel Coward wrote it,"[21] began Brooks Atkinson in reviewing the 1957 American production of
Nude with Violin, and that fact remains the play's claim
to enduring importance. The Princess Anya's slavic im-
periousness and Cherry-May Waterton's cockney bravura
provide fine theatrical moments, and Sebastien's two-
faced propriety is an actor's joy, but the play is little
more than an array of such comic characterizations. Like
the great bulk of forgotten stage comedies, *Nude with
Violin* fails because characterization is indulged to the
neglect of plot. It is a peculiarly amateur mistake for The
Master to have made as his career drew to a close.

4

The Melodramas

Although Coward is most often associated with the comedy of manners, light comedy, and musical comedy, his oeuvre is not limited to those genres. Melodramas form a large part of his work for the stage, from *The Vortex* in 1924 to *A Song at Twilight* in 1966, and it was the melodramatic scenes of *Cavalcade* as much as the repartee of *Private Lives* that established him as the premier British playwright of the 1930s. If contemporaries were persistent in their view of him as a comic writer, they also congratulated him regularly on the seriousness of his melodramas. Coward himself seems to have been indifferent to considerations of genre. The crispness that makes his comedic dialogue so vibrant is the strength of his melodramatic dialogue as well, and he was as proud of the one as of the other.

Coward's sense of melodrama was formed by the Edwardian theater and owes a natural debt to the elaborately contrived situations and stirring "curtains" of such dramatists as Henry Arthur Jones and Arthur Wing Pinero. Almost as important is his debt to the "problem" play of Ibsen and Shaw. He liked to tell the story of attending the theater with an actress who said, "If it's a play with a message, I shan't dress," but among the subjects of his melodramas are such problem-play themes as drug addiction, homosexuality, nymphomania, the breakdown of the class system, and the human cost of war. Coward cared more that his plays were theatrically effective than that they were intellectually provocative,[1] but Ibsen and Shaw proved to him that social problems make good melodrama. The result is a range of plays that can loosely be termed "melodramatic"—plays melodramatic in style but with problem-play subjects, plays melodramatic in plotting but understated in style, and plays melodramatic in subject but intellectual in approach.

With few exceptions, Coward's melodramas are now period pieces. Time has blunted their sensationalism and outmoded their contrivances, and only a handful of his later plays are staged today. Among the best of his melodramas, however, *The Vortex* and *Easy Virtue* retain the interest of the sensation they were in their day, and *Post-Mortem* compels serious attention for its technique. *Peace in Our Time* and *This Happy Breed* are noteworthy for catching The Master in a proletarian mood, and *Waiting in the Wings* and *A Song at Twilight* merit interest for their climaxing of a distinguished career.

The Vortex

Like all of Coward's early plays, *The Vortex* had to go the round of theatrical managements for several months with attendant indignities for its author. The producer H. M. Harwood said he would consider the play only if Coward agreed not to play the lead. "As one of my principal objects in writing the play had been to give myself a first-rate opportunity for dramatic acting," Coward reported icily, "I refused his offer."[2] The manager of a small repertory theater subsequently expressed interest in mounting a production, and after a wrangle with the Lord Chamberlain about licensing, *The Vortex* opened in darkest Hampstead on November 25, 1924. The beau monde was in full attendance, stirred to curiosity by the Lord Chamberlain's misgivings. Michael Arlen was there, Lady Louis Mountbattan and Sir Edward Marsh as well, and the glitter of diamonds in the audience is said to have been so dazzling that no one noticed the coconut matting underfoot. When the curtain came down, it was clear that London had its major play of the season. Other managements were quick to make bids, and after twelve performances in the Hampstead theater, *The Vortex* moved to the West End, where it shocked and titillated London for 224 performances. As its playwright, director, and principal actor, twenty-three-year-old Coward was established overnight as a theatrical wunderkind.

   The Vortex begins in Florence Lancaster's London flat as two of her friends, Helen Saville and Pawnie Quentin, wait for her to return. The two friends wonder what will become of Florence — whether she can go on seeming young forever and attracting athletic young gigolos like Tom Veryan, whose photograph is prominently displayed in Florence's sitting room. The situation must be trying for her husband David, and fiendish for her twenty-four-year-old son Nicky, speculates Pawnie. Another friend, Clara Hibbert, enters, closely followed by Florence herself with Tom Veryan in tow. Helen tries to warn Florence that Tom is not in love with her and observes that one must grow old when the time comes. Florence's outrage is stifled by the arrival of Nicky, just back from a year spent studying music in Paris. Obviously devoted to his glamorous mother, Nicky is nevertheless pale and nervous in dealing with her, especially in explaining that he is engaged to a girl named Bunty Mainwaring, whom he introduces. Tom and Bunty already know each other, as it happens. They are, in fact, old lovers.

   Act II takes place the following weekend at the Lancaster's country home, where a house party is noisily in progress. Florence embarrasses her guests by her irritation with the gentle David, quarrels with Tom, and tries to stir up trouble between Helen and David, then between Nicky and Bunty. She is too self-centered to notice Nicky's state of nerves, and only Helen deduces the truth—that Nicky is addicted to drugs. Nicky is further unnerved when Bunty breaks off their engagement in a breezy, modern way, and emotions come to a head when Florence and Nicky discover Bunty and Tom locked in an embrace. Florence orders the treacherous lovers from her house, while Nicky tries to drown the scene with jazz syncopations played fortissimo on the piano.

Act III is set in Florence's bedroom later the same night. Helen is consoling a distraught Florence but also trying to make her see Tom's desertion as inevitable. Nicky interrupts, and after Helen has left he forces Florence to admit that Tom has been her lover—that all the stories he has tried not to believe about her are true. He has grown up all wrong, he says. It is not her fault, Florence whines. *Of course* it is her fault, he replies brutally. He claims to see for the first time how really old she is, despite the imposture of fair hair and painted face. Finally confessing his addiction, he sweeps her cosmetics off the dressing table and tells her that her career as the youthful Florence Lancaster is over. She is going to be the mother he needs before he goes over the edge of sanity completely. The curtain comes down on a tableau of shared anguish and despair.

The tremor that ran through London and New York audiences when Nicky Lancaster admitted to being a drug addict was like a seismic shock. The theater thrives on sensation, and a young man of conventionally good family declaring himself an addict onstage was unquestionably sensational in 1924, although drugs were by no means unfamiliar to sophisticated playgoers, and practically everyone in London and New York society knew of *someone* who had sampled marijuana or cocaine.[3] That Nicky is in the early stages of addiction, that he is eager to break his dependence on drugs, and that the tone adopted toward his habit is one of unalloyed horror did little to mitigate a sense that one of society's dark secrets had been unveiled. James Agate, the dean of London reviewers, spoke for many when he observed that Coward's play was stamped with "the imprint of truth."[4]

The relationship between mother and son in the play was also thought a terrible imprint of truth. One suspects that the Mayfair parents who forbade their sons and daughters to attend the play were of similar mind to "Honest" Abe Erlanger, an American producer of the play who would not permit his name to appear on programs because he thought the third act disparaged motherhood. The Freudian aspects of the mother-son relationship contributed especially to the audiences' sense of awful truths being disclosed. Nicky's fascination with his mother's beauty is clearly an Oedipal fixation, and Florence's penchant for young men is vaguely nymphomaniacal, certainly neurotic. When Nicky remarks that *of course* it is his mother's fault, mothers everywhere felt besieged, and their offspring, liberated — not just by the Freudian gloss but by the casual, presumptive logic. That *of course* mothers were to blame was really the play's most sensational statement.

Mothers were always of great interest to Coward, from the irrepressible Judith Bliss of *Hay Fever* to Mrs. Wentworth-Brewster, ensconced in "A Bar on the Piccola Marina" and rejecting her children's plea to "Please come home, Mama." Although he admired the life-force of such women, Coward admonished that "The pleasures that once were heaven / Look silly at sixty-seven," and in some form or another he always raised the question that he formulated most memorably in song:

> Hush-a-bye, hush-a-bye, hush-a-bye, my darlings,
> Try not to fret and wet your cots,
> One day you'll clench your tiny fists
> And murder your psychiatrists,
> What's, what's, what's going to happen to the tots?

Nicky Lancaster is a major example of what happens to such tots, but Coward's picture of the emotional damage done Nicky is too thin to be really convincing.[5] That Nicky is in love with his mother is clear, but it is not at all clear how his infatuation with Bunty Mainwaring qualifies, enters into, or manifests that love. Nor is it clear how his affection for his father is consistent with an Oedipal fixation. One understands Nicky's instinctive dislike of Tom Veryan, for Tom is a rival for his mother's affection, but the overlaying of that rivalry with a more substantial rivalry focused on Bunty Mainwaring trivializes the incestuous theme and reduces the Freudian dynamics of the play from a serious to a simply melodramatic interest.

The play's Freudianism is less compelling today than its rendering of 1920s society: the nervous vitality of the jazz generation, the brittle conversation, the drift to despair. The exits and entrances in the play are sudden and erratic, eminently suited to the restlessness of the characters, and the telephone that rings repeatedly in Act I seems the pulse of society, interrupting conversations and sounding the note of modern busyness. Florence complains that her house has the atmosphere of a railway station, but she clearly fosters that atmosphere and crams her days to the point of bursting. A series of comic scenes that develops a theme of rudeness suggests especially this frenzy of modern life. Even kindly persons like Pawnie and Helen are compelled by life's momentum to deal in rudeness, as a kind of attitudinal shorthand.

Verbal exchanges in the play are so staccato that they seem a musical extension of Nicky's jazz piano. Like the impulsive exits and entrances, the exchanges are characterized by sudden and willful shifts of focus that suggest Coward's people live on the edge of hysteria, deathly fearful that truth will be spoken unless it is conversationally aborted. In an effort to give weight to their speech, these lost souls affect the hyperbolic style of fash-

ionable Mayfair and deal in expressions like "divine,"
"too thrilling," and "too perfectly marvelous." Evasions
dominate the effect of such phrases.

Evasiveness is also the keynote of a scene like that
in which Florence and Nicky first meet after a long
separation. Indeed, the scene is compelling largely *because* of its evasions. Florence remarks compulsively on
her youthful appearance in order to override a minor
disagreement with Nicky, and Helen decides to leave at
that point, apparently unwilling to indulge Florence's
vanity. Nicky's hope that Helen will stay longer suggests
a fear of being alone with his mother, emphasized by his
greater ease with Helen; and Helen's speculation that
Florence may not be speaking to her by the weekend
suggests an awareness of what Florence will make of her
admonition that one must finally admit to growing old.
When Nicky remarks on the familiarity of the domestic
scene, it is probable that he is referring to the tangled
web Florence throws over her current irritation with
Helen. In shifting away from the subject of Helen, however, Florence assumes opportunistically that Nicky is
turning the conversation to pleasantries. The point of the
scene is that neither mother nor son has the courage to
pursue the subject of their relationship — upon which the
conversational vectors threaten to converge.

The scene in Act II in which the assembled characters dance to gramophone and piano music develops
further the sense of fractured, frenetic lives. Florence's
complaint in Act I that she and Nicky have lost the knack
of dancing with one another stands as background to the
scene and prepares us to understand its suggestion that
the elegant measures of the fox-trot cannot soothe the
disquiet of postwar relationships. The music is much too
fast, complains Helen. Pawnie murmurs in turn that she
has never danced well since the war, and Florence is
soon accusing Tom of dancing abominably. Coward's
staging of the scene calls for a feeling of feverish amuse-

ment, the air thick with cigarette smoke and superlatives, and the lines timed to reach the audience as the
speakers pass near the footlights in their dancing. The
effect is a flashing montage of conversational moments,
a cinematic technique suited admirably both to the restlessness of the characters and to the play's mood of aggressive modernity. The brokenness of the dialogue culminates in Tom's breaking with Florence and Bunty's
breaking with Nicky and culminates ultimately in the
breakdown of mother and son at the final curtain. Indeed, brokenness is the burden of contemporary life in
The Vortex — at least among those who, in Nicky's words,
"swirl about in a vortex of beastliness."

Because it deals superficially with most of its themes,
The Vortex is melodrama rather than a Shavian problem
play. But if the suggestions of nymphomania in Florence,
of repressed love in Helen, of banked fires of decency in
David, and of an Oedipal complex in Nicky fail to coalesce as rhetoric, it is precisely their failure to coalesce,
combined with the brittle conversations and the sudden
veerings of plot, that give *The Vortex* its period distinction. Few plays of its time capture so well a sense that
the jazz generation had opened Pandora's Box and that
nothing would ever again be the same. Few plays of the
time capture so well the terrible despair of the Bright
Young Things. There is no peace anywhere, Nicky avers,
only the unending din of desperate amusement.

Easy Virtue

Easy Virtue was written in 1924, shortly after the writing of *The Vortex*, and it first saw production in America, where it ran for several months despite criticism that
it was "a flash rather than a play."[6] Brought to the London stage in 1926, it ran once again for only several
months, and British reviewers were no more impressed

than their American counterparts. "Mr. Noel Coward gets younger with every play," wrote James Agate in the London *Sunday Times*, "and in *Easy Virtue* has attained to that pure idealism which prompts the schoolboy who has been taken to see *La Dame aux Camélias* to believe for the next ten years that a *cocotte* is the noblest work of man if not of God."[7]

Easy Virtue is certainly in the tradition of *La dame aux camélias*, although Pinero's *The Second Mrs. Tanqueray* is its more immediate prototype. The play is set in the home of Colonel and Mrs. Whittaker and their children Marion, Hilda, and John. They are a wealthy English family, devoted (except for the colonel) to the pursuits of country life. In the opening act, the Whittakers await the arrival of newly wed John and his cosmopolitan wife Larita, whom they have never met. Marion and Mrs. Whittaker's worst suspicions are realized when Larita proves to be not only older than John but divorced, and a notable chill pervades her welcome. The colonel greets Larita warmly, however, as does Sarah Hurst, a neighbor whom John had been expected to marry. Larita behaves impeccably, for she is both sophisticated and sensitive.

Act II begins three months later, and it is immediately clear that Larita is at odds with the household. She lies on a sofa reading Proust's *Sodom and Gomorrah* as first Mrs. Whittaker, then Marion, and finally John encourage her halfheartedly to be more vigorous. Only the colonel realizes how deeply she is bored by country-house life, and only he tries to relieve her tedium with jokes and conversation. Most upsetting to Larita is her husband's neglect, for she sincerely loves John and knows he is no longer in love with her. At tea, a hysterical Hilda produces an old newspaper clipping that implicates Larita in a man's suicide and contains a list of her alleged lovers. A quarrel ensues that results in Mrs. Whittaker's request that Larita remain upstairs during a supper dance that evening. The message is clear: Larita is not welcome in decent society. Left alone at the curtain, Larita breaks down. She throws *Sodom and Gomorrah* at a reproduction of the Venus de Milo and collapses on the sofa, weeping uncontrolledly.

Act III takes place during Mrs. Whittaker's dance, which is conventionally tedious until Larita makes a late appearance, sensationally bejeweled and painted. The soul of restraint until this climactic moment, she suddenly adopts as her own Marion's practice of speaking the unvarnished truth. In an effort to cover her social embarrassment, Mrs. Whittaker claims to have understood that Larita was indisposed with a headache, but Larita snaps back that her claim is quite untrue — that she understood nothing of the kind. When Mrs. Whittaker continues her pretense, unable to adjust to her daughter-in-law's new boldness, Larita gives no quarter and asks why she persists in the ridiculous notion that she was ill. John is sent away coolly when he objects to Larita's appearance, and a young man who has wagered she will dance with him is summarily dismissed. It is to Sarah Hurst that the scarlet woman confesses her intention to leave John and the Whittaker house that evening. Sarah is fond of him, she says, and in the right order of things ought to have married him. Quietly, the dance still in full swing, she takes her leave with only the butler in attendance.

Coward made an unconvincing effort in 1947 to redeem the old-fashioned theatrics of *Easy Virtue* by hinting it was actually a comedy misplayed over the years as melodrama.[8] He averred more credibly a year or two later that it was written in a mood of nostalgia for social graces that fell victim during the twenties to a cult of energy.[9] The saucy rejoinder and the indifferent shrug of the shoulders, the use of profanity in the drawing room, the insouciance of the fancy dress "do" and the game called Treasure Hunt — all were trademarks of a decade that valued boldness and high energy more than Larita's quiet charm. *Easy Virtue* is nostalgic, as Coward claimed, in that it disparages this cult of energy and celebrates such unfashionable virtues as civility and restraint. Larita's triumph over Mrs. Whittaker and her offspring is a triumph of modern sexual freedom over old-fashioned prudery, assuredly, but it is more importantly a triumph of old-fashioned sensitivity over modern boorishness, of good manners over bad, and of real virtue, however "easy," over cant.

Of course Larita is not really a woman of easy virtue at all. She has never had an affair with a man she wasn't fond of, she says proudly; the only time she ever sold herself was in a church marriage to her first husband. Secure in her virtue, she makes no other effort to defend her conduct in the past, as she makes no effort to lay a burden of guilt upon John for the failure of their marriage. Until driven to her grand gesture in Act III, she treats the weightiest truths with a lightness that betokens her grace of mind and character. When John asks why she is not happy, she explains very simply that he has stopped loving her. John is shocked by her candor and protests that he hasn't stopped loving her — to which she responds with affecting lightness, "Liar!"

Larita, however, is not wholly convincing as one more-sinned-against-than-sinning, for she eventually puts aside her restraint and sensitivity in order to deal more effectively with the Whittaker women. Her eloquence once she is launched in debate with Mrs. Whittaker is startling, and her marksmanship as a rhetorician is surprising in one so sensitive to feelings as she. "Huh!" Marion snorts contemptuously when Larita questions the validity of marriages contracted by the very young, and Larita enquires immediately what she might mean by such a peculiar noise. Is it an expression of approval, of contempt, or merely of asthma? When Mrs. Whittaker charges her daughter-in-law with being a wicked, wicked woman, Larita surrenders no argumentative ground and labels the accusation both fatuous and mechanical. Her mother-in-law didn't even think before she said it, Larita observes coolly. Even nineteen-year-old Hilda, distraught at what she has caused with her newspaper clipping, is given no quarter. Larita responds to her plea for forgiveness by enjoining her not to be a toad — to have at least the courage of her convictions.

Nor is Larita wholly convincing when she comments in the manner of a Shavian heroine on the Whittakers as a social phenomenon. For all her denunciations of their false values, she deals superficially in accusations of bigotry, priggishness, and repressed sexual impulses, which are at best the dark underside of values she leaves unspecified. Dramaturgically, the Whittakers' values seem innocuous: an undue respect for convention, for heartiness, and for dogs. We have only Larita's implied insight as evidence that heartiness on the tennis court engenders bigotry in the heart, that conventional forthrightness conceals darkly Freudian repressions. Indeed, Larita's suggestion that Marion's air of heartiness is spurious and masks a need for love and affection is 1920s psychologizing of the most facile kind.

Coward seems to have intended Colonel Whittaker to reinforce Larita's judgments, inasmuch as he shares her distaste for the schoolgirl code by which his wife and daughters live. He is relieved when Mrs. Whittaker becomes cross, he remarks to Marion, inasmuch as he prefers irritability to hysteria. When Marion suggests patronizingly that the colonel's bitterness is born of unhappiness, he asks disingenuously if she wants to have a "straight talk" with him. He shares Larita's esteem for Proust and her disesteem for his wife's palpitations, and he shares her distaste for people like Marion who affiliate themselves with the Almighty.

Yet the colonel's equanimity has the effect of undercutting Larita's rebellion in the play. He is regarded by the women in his family as an unregenerate cad, just as they regard Larita as an unregenerate coquette, but he deals with such opprobrium by refusing to show himself disturbed. Larita's overdressing like a courtesan for the dance seems a melodramatic gesture in comparison with his studied calmness, and her stooping to challenge Marion's and Mrs. Whittaker's contempt for her seems an indulgence compared to the colonel's sustained refusal to defend himself against their contempt — all the more so in that she ignores their contempt for so long. In short, the colonel represents for the audience all that is admirable in British reticence. Because Larita's more Continental mode of reticence is shattered, she seems less firmly grounded than the colonel in important ways.

What makes the play good melodrama is precisely these discrepancies between Larita's cultivated restraint and her grand gesture, between what we see the Whittaker women to be on the surface and Larita's vision of their grisly depths, between Colonel Whittaker as an exemplar and Larita as something less than the ideal. Such contrasts are the lifeblood of melodrama, and they are almost as theatrically stirring as the sight of Larita descending the stairs to the ballroom in a daringly cut gown, wearing every piece of jewelry she owns. Shaw's complaint about *The Second Mrs. Tanqueray* — that the tragedy does not develop from character but from a situation — is applicable no less to *Easy Virtue* as *Tanqueray*'s offspring, but like Pinero, Coward extracts good theater from a situation that Shaw and Ibsen used to indict society. As James Agate found cause to remark on reviewing the play's London opening, theater is, after all, theater.[10] *Easy Virtue* has the "easy" but theatrical virtues of its melodramatic kind: suspense, vivid moral contrasts, and a thrillingly lurid great scene.

Post-Mortem

The most unrelievedly serious of Coward's melodramas is *Post-Mortem*, a war play written in 1930 in the midst of a spate of war novels best exemplified by Hemingway's *A Farewell to Arms* and Remarque's *All Quiet on the Western Front*. *Post-Mortem* was partially inspired by such novels, but it was inspired more immediately by Coward's playing the role of Stanhope in a run of R. C. Sherriff's *Journey's End*, a grimly realistic play about life in the trenches. Alexander Woollcott and other Coward friends were firm in their opinion that *Post-Mortem* was not in The Master's best mode and argued successfully against its production. Influenced by their opinion, probably, Coward labeled the work "an angry little vilification of war," "confused," "shallow," "hysterical," "muddled," a purge of "certain accumulated acids" in his system.[11] Critics have generally taken their cue from this disapprobation,[12] but prisoners of war at Oflag VIIb in Eichstatt, Germany, found the play more estimable and gave it the first known production in 1944. On rereading the text in 1956, Coward also found *Post-Mortem* better than he had thought. "On looking back I think that it was foolish of me not to have had it produced at the time," he wrote. "It is wise to listen to other people's opinions but not always wise to be guided by them."[13]

A play in eight scenes, *Post-Mortem* interfolds two different time schemes set thirteen years apart. The first and last scenes are set in a company headquarters on the front line in 1917, and the intervening scenes take place in various settings in and about London in 1930. In Scene 1, Officers Tilley, Shaw, Robins, and Lomas express various degrees of humor and indignation over a London newspaper's pathologic patriotism. They forget momentarily that among them is John Cavan, son of the newspaper's publisher, but John is not distressed in any obvious way by the fatuities of the *Daily Mercury*. Philosophical by nature, he expresses the hope that years from now the world will have learned something from the war. Shortly thereafter he is shot (offstage) by an enemy sniper and carried back to company headquarters. Dying, he says he will know now if his hopes for the future are valid.

In six subsequent scenes, John's ghost appears to his mother, Lady Cavan; to his fiancée, Monica Chellerton; to his fellow officer, Perry Lomas; to his father, Sir James Cavan; to a gathering of his former comrades Shaw, Tilley, and Robins; and finally to his mother again. Only the living have experienced the thirteen-year interval since the war. As John enters and exits each of these scenes, guns fire in the background and voices echo from the first scene, suggesting that John has been catapulted into the future while still on his deathbed. As he talks in 1930 with those still dear to him, he perceives not the bright new world he had hoped for but a world run aground on cant and venality— a world not worthy of the war's carnage. He sees the terrible loneliness of Lady Cavan, the shallow life of his unhappily married fiancée, the despair of Perry Lomas, the utter opportunism of his father, the mean accommodations his comrades have made in peacetime. As stretcher-bearers approach John's pallet in the last scene, he opens his eyes one last time before he dies and murmurs to Perry Lomas that the cynics are right— that the war is a poor joke.

Post-Mortem is remarkable primarily for its tone. Although ostensibly a ghost play, it avoids gothicism completely. When John's ghost appears to his friends and family, they are agreeably surprised for the most part but not startled. Lord and Lady Cavan treat John not as a specter but as a prodigal son, and Perry Lomas even puts John off for several moments in the hope that his ghostly visitor will disappear. The effect of such aplomb in the face of the supernatural is dreamlike, quashing all aspects of the situation that might appear to be sensational. This aplomb also has the effect of subsuming the six apparition scenes into John's death-bed consciousness, for the ease with which others accept his apparition thirteen years after his death seems a spillover of the aplomb that characterizes John's own attitudes. Indeed, *Post-Mortem* is as credibly a psychological play as a ghost play, and its subject can be understood equally well as a death-bed vision or as a series of ghostly visitations.

In the context of this untroubling ambiguity of time and ontology, the troubledness of the people John visits seems petulance — a failure to perceive the larger concerns of human existence that John hoped the war would clarify. Monica Chellerton refuses to talk about a boring war over and done with and asks John how dare he judge her, as he died young and hadn't time to find out about everything being a bore. Perry complains of a hopelessness not quite despair, a boredom in which everything is whittled down to essentials that aren't there. Other characters seem humanly eroded, wizened by the postwar years. John asks Shaw if he has children and Shaw snaps resentfully that he should mind his own business. He asks Robins if the memory of a beloved comrade had stayed with him, and Robins snorts indignantly that he is talking rot. Even the gracious Lady Cavan is imprisoned in loneliness. No one seems able to break out of his private emptiness into what John calls the "splendid carelessness" of the war — by which he means liberation from the ephemeral and the exaggerated.

If the characters cannot break out of their emptiness, John's ghostliness enables him to break into their emptiness, and in a series of break-ins increasingly irrealistic, the play builds to its climax. John catches Perry Lomas in Scene 4 preparing to commit suicide, not just because his book about the war has been attacked by the *Daily Mercury* with hysterical outrage, but because he cannot live humiliated by the simple fact of being alive. His problem is *nerves*, insists John, who even during the war thought Perry on the verge of mental breakdown. But Perry's catalogue of postwar ills — poverty, unemployment, pain, greed, cruelty, passion, crime — persuades John that Perry is a greater idealist than he, and in a sanctioning gesture he hands Perry a revolver. As the suicide shot rings out, it overlays the shot that killed

John in scene 1, and we hear Perry say to Shaw over John's body that the wounded man is not quite unconscious — that he opened his eyes. A measure of John's tenacious idealism dies in Perry's death, we understand, a development measured by John's eyes opening to Perry's vision.

In Scene 5, John surprises his father at a meeting convened to denounce Perry Lomas's book, and the catalogue of postwar ills from Scene 4 is raised to the level of surrealistic farce. Alfred Borrow, city editor of the *Mercury*, speaks in frantic journalese. Miss Beaver, a primly efficient secretary, slips in and out of hysteria that no one notices. The doddering Bishop of Ketchworth is ready to censor Lomas's book under the impression that it deals with the rape of a little girl in a country lane. Lord Cavan listens to his son toast him as a liar, a hypocrite, a robber baron, a political cheat, and a licentious sentimentalist and responds madly with heartfelt thanks.

The characters never really hear each others' words in this scene, so immersed are they in platitudes, and John cannot break through their smug assumptions about what is being said, no matter how accusatory his rhetoric. That the bishop and Lord Cavan are recognizable caricatures of the reigning Bishop of London in 1930 and the newspaper magnate Lord Beaverbrook deepens the sense of surrealistic farce. "Long live War!" John finally declaims, arguing that death, destruction and despair offer promise of something clearer and sweeter than anything the bloody gods of Lord Cavan and the bishop have ever offered. "God and Country" chant the others, mindlessly. As the moral darkness of the meeting fades into the darkness of the front, we hear Perry say of the dying John, "I think he opened his eyes."

Scene 6 plunges so deeply into the darkness of the present that John is able to call forth the younger selves of Robins and Shaw from the shadows of memory. Those young selves take up position behind their older selves on the stage in a solemn suggestion that something clearer and sweeter than the present might yet be distilled from the experience of the war. But Tilley refuses to be drawn forth and castigates John for what he understands to be sentimental revisionism. Refusing to remember John's memories, intending to forget this dream even before his eyes open, Tilley virtually hounds John from the stage and from the year 1930. Tilley stands for the obdurateness of the age and the foolishness of John's hope that the human cost of the war might have purchased something worthwhile for civilization. Coward is not clear what that something is, and critics are right when they accuse the play of being rhetorically hollow, but it is fitting that what might have been should remain unspecified, for it is Coward's point that it is undiscovered.

The measure of *Post-Mortem*'s sophistication is that it is not, like so many other war plays, an embarrassment years after it was written. Its play of sentiment against disillusion and of coolness against passion is intellectually durable, and its simultaneous vision of the war's present-tense integrity and past-tense futility is both dramaturgically and culturally impressive. None of Coward's plays have been so undervalued as *Post-Mortem*, and none suggest more forcefully the untapped depths of his talent for melodrama.

Peace in Our Time

There are varying accounts of how *Peace in Our Time* came to be written. Because the play deals with a Nazi occupation following upon an imaginary defeat of England in World War II, and because H. H. Munro (or "Saki") was one of Coward's favorite writers, Cole Lesley suggests the influence of *When William Came*, Munro's fantasy about a German occupation of England during the first World War.[14] Coward's diary, however, suggests that the idea for such a play came to him quite out of the blue in 1946.[15] In 1958 Coward claimed still another origin: that the idea for *Peace in Our Time* first came to him in 1944 shortly after the liberation of Paris from the Nazis.[16]

Whatever its first inspiration, *Peace in Our Time* takes as its theme what might have happened had Germany won the Battle of Britain. Set entirely in the saloon bar of a London public house named The Shy Gazelle, it charts the course of a Nazi occupation from November 1940 to May 1945 and the concurrent development of a resistance movement. Fred and Nora Shattock run the pub, assisted first by their daughter Doris and then by a barmaid named Phyllis Mere. The Shattock's son Stevie has been reported killed in action some months before the start of the play, but he has actually been confined in a French prison camp. Among the pub's regular customers are Lyia Vivian, a cabaret "artiste"; George Bourne, her lover; Mr. and Mrs. Grainger, an elderly couple whose son is in a concentration camp on the Isle of Wight; Janet Braid, a novelist whose son was killed in the war; Alma Boughton, a commercial buyer; and Chorley Bannister, a collaborationist who edits a highbrow journal called *Progress*. A minor German official named Albrecht Richter is an occasional, unwelcome customer.

As the play progresses, the German occupation turns increasingly ugly, and unhappiness about shortages and forced relocations gives way to rumors about arrests, beatings, and disappearances. The Graingers' son Billy and the Shattocks' son Stevie escape their separate prison camps and arrive in London determined to serve the resistance. Soon The Shy Gazelle and its patrons make up part of a resistance cell: George Bourne becomes the cell's leader; Fred, Nora, Lyia, Doris, Billy, and Stevie are among the members; and the Shattock pub serves as a meeting place until Chorley Bannister betrays it to

Richter. On the eve of an Allied invasion, Richter arrests
and tortures Doris, and she dies refusing to implicate her
comrades. In retaliation, several members of the resistance kidnap Richter and hold him at The Shy Gazelle
for mock trial and summary execution. Before they can
proceed, however, Nazi troops who have discovered
Richter's whereabouts fire through the door of the pub
and kill their countryman inadvertently. Simultaneously, we hear a radio broadcast that implies the liberation
has begun.

Peace in Our Time is less sensational than this plot
summary might suggest, for its emphasis is on the gradual adjustment of ordinary English men and women to
the fact of German occupation. The melodramatic deaths
of Doris and Richter are less typical of the play than a
carefully measured decline in the quality of beer available in The Shy Gazelle, and the arrest of Jews on Edg-
ware Road receives less attention than the onus of licensing hours. Gestapo agents circulate through the pub
twice, demanding identification papers, but a plucky
old woman who heads a resistance cell in Kent is a more
formidable stage presence. In short, the occupation is
background in the play, and the drama of ordinary life
under the occupation is foreground. The German con-
quest is not even made clear until the end of the first
scene, although remarks that "they" have requisitioned
Queen's Hotel and that the trains are being run with perfect efficiency hint at the eventual disclosure.

Peace in Our Time is remarkable primarily for its
picture of human spirits rising and falling under the
pressures of foreign domination. Fred's initial stance in
the play is one of weary disillusion — even of bitterness —
that he had believed Chamberlain's promise there would
be "peace in our time." People who adjust to the German victory are sensible, he suggests, for life has to go
on. But when Albrecht Richter asks him somewhat later
in the play how long it will take ordinary Englishmen

like Fred to become reconciled to the situation, Fred answers that they will never be reconciled — neither they, nor their children, nor their children's children. In terms of plot, this is not so much heroism as a variation in Fred's mood. In another scene he senses that Nora is becoming resistant to the new political order and enjoins her to be careful what she does, careful what she says, even careful what she thinks. Yet when Nora tries to discourage her children from working for the resistance, Fred tries gently to embolden her and tells her she doesn't really mean what she is saying. Fred and Nora keep each other going in this mutually supportive way, and they come to stand for a kind of courage that is stronger for knowing weariness.

Alma Boughton is also a study in courage that ebbs and flows. Raising her glass early in the play, she cannot bring herself to say "Happy Days," yet she argues with desperate logic a few minutes later that she is gratified England lost the Battle of Britain. With victory, she says, England would have become lazy again, whereas in defeat the country still has a chance. There will be no time now for class wars and industrial crises and political squabbles, she says. British men and women will have to be united until they have driven the enemy away and cleansed themselves again. Under the influence of a brandy, Alma alarms everyone in Act I by announcing flippantly that she is plotting the overthrow of the Third Reich, but in Act II she is aghast when her mother lifts a glass and cries, "Down with Hitler!" Alcoholic courage endangers others, she admonishes the old woman, as she herself had to be admonished earlier.

Minor characters reinforce this eminently human variety, sometimes comically. In her passion for the cinema, the barmaid Phyllis goes to see German propaganda films as readily as British and American films, but she is sweetly mindless about their content and confutes Fred's melodramatic fear that she will be influenced by what she sees. Alfie Blake explains to his wife Lily that before the invasion the Allied Command will send over aircraft to weaken Germany's coastal defenses, and Lily asks naïvely if he means they will drop bombs. What does she imagine they will drop, he asks — licorice candies? In the next scene, aircraft are heard overhead and Alfie comments that they sound like fighter bombers. With her husband's own irascibility, Lily asks what else they would be likely to send — sewing machines? Of such counterpoint are human relationships constructed in *Peace in Our Time*, and of such changeable temper is human nature constituted.

So authentic is the ring of these changes in the play that the unflagging heroism of Stevie and Doris tends to ring false. If *Peace in Our Time* were a wartime composition, Stevie's curtain-line speech about the hope for which they are all working would be appropriately inspiriting, but in the postwar period, its pieties recall too well the formulaic optimism to which the majority of war plays reduced the complexity of wartime awarenesses. Similarly, Janet's extravagant contempt for Chorley's intellectual accommodations is too pat in a postwar drama, too ex post facto. In the second act, Janet pays a climactic tribute to Fred in equally extravagant terms, and even though we understand that she is praising Fred less than she is praising the genus *Englishman*, her extravagance rings false simply because *Peace in Our Time* has no postwar need to flatter the national character in this way.

The climactic moments of the play are given over to such inspirational rhetoric nonetheless, and it seems likely that at least part of Coward's intention was to stir his audience to patriotic fervor. Indeed, it can be seen as the play's failure that it has an unplayable mix of wartime passions and postwar disenchantments. This mix can be played as a strength, however, inasmuch as it is a particularly apt formula for suggesting the emotional range of an occupied people. The war is both over and not-over for the denizens of The Shy Gazelle, and their variant and variable responses to the occupation compose a stageworthy, antiheroic picture of unexpectedly heroic men and women whose spirits sometimes flag, whose heads are sometimes bowed, and whose rhetoric is simply realistic — however excessive — when victory seems theirs. I have argued before that among the unacknowledged strengths of Coward's plays is a shrewd sense of psychology when frustration bites deeply into the human soul. Like *Post-Mortem*, written so many years before it, *Peace in Our Time* is stageable because of that psychological strength.

Cavalcade

Although it is generally forgotten today, *Cavalcade* (1931) suggests better than any of his plays how thoroughly Coward understood stagecraft and production values. An awesome undertaking for its time, it is a play of twenty-two scenes and sixteen different sets, involves forty principals and hundreds of bit players, necessitates an inordinate number of costumes (Coward calculated the number at 3,700),[17] makes such a complex use of hydraulic lifts that it was widely assumed to employ a revolving stage,[18] and requires such troublesome props as a full-scale locomotive. So reluctant was the locomotive to advance on cue during rehearsals that stagehands christened it "the Shy Virgin," but in all else the production bore witness to Coward's organizational genius. Indeed, such logistics suggest that *Cavalcade* was The Master's answer to a fashionable view that the stage had to defer to the cinema in terms of spectacle. Like *Post-Mortem*, it seems also to have been an attempt to match onstage the freedom of time and space enjoyed by motion pictures.

Basically a historical play, *Cavalcade* moves breezily from New Year's Eve, 1899, to an evening in 1930,
touching en route such milestones of emotional history
as the Boer War, the relief of the British garrison at
Mafeking in South Africa after a siege of 217 days, the
death of Queen Victoria, Doctor Crippen, the sinking
of the *Titanic*, the development of the airplane, and the
long haul of World War I. The idea for the play came
to Coward while perusing bound volumes of *Black and
White* and the *Illustrated London News*, and it retains
in execution much of its journalistic inspiration. Cockney
newsboys call out the great events offstage, and parlor-
maids dash out to buy halfpenny papers while ladies and
gentlemen move to drawing-room windows to hear the
latest headlines. Few of the great events are seen first-
hand, but they loom always in the background.

In the foreground of the play are two families. The
upper classes are represented by Robert and Jane Marroyt
(who become Lord and Lady Marryot halfway through
the play) and their sons Edward and Joe. The lower
classes are represented by Alfred and Ellen Bridges, originally butler and parlormaid to the Marryots, but after 1901 the owners of a public house. Their daughter
Fanny, who becomes a successful chanteuse sometime
around 1918, enjoys a liaison with Joe that suggests the
gradual breakdown of class distinctions in Britain.

Through moments in these characters' lives resound
the headline stories of thirty years. We glimpse the Boer
War in the departures of Robert Marryot and Alfred
Bridges on the same troopship and in a patriotic music-
hall sketch witnessed by Jane and her friend Margaret
Harris. Queen Victoria's death is commemorated by an
unseen funeral procession passing beneath the Marryots'
windows. Edward Marryot and his bride set sail in 1912
on the *Titanic*, wondering ironically if their love will
last. Joe Marryot asks Fanny Bridges to marry him as he
departs for the war front in 1914, and a tearful Jane

Marryot joins a crowd in Trafalgar Square to celebrate an armistice superimposed on news of Joe's death. The net effect is of lives lived in highlight: of the upper classes moving downscale and of the lower classes moving upscale, of war's increasing madness, of young promise crushed and old dignities maintained, all in the flickering light of time accelerated.

When a deeply moved audience thundered its approval at the end of *Cavalcade*'s first-night performance, Coward was summoned to the stage and made an impromptu speech which concluded with the statement, "I hope that this play has made you feel that, in spite of the troublous times we are living in, it is still pretty exciting to be English."[19] Although isolating the strand of Victorian patriotism in the play and ignoring other strands of meaning, the remark appealed to an audience already stirred by national efforts to overcome the Depression and worried by the country's imminent abandonment of the gold standard. The result was a widespread perception of *Cavalcade* as a call to patriotism. In Coward's own phrase, it was perceived as "theatrically effective jingoism."[20] "The note of national pride pervading every scene and every sentence must make each one of us face the future with courage and high hopes," rhapsodized the *Daily Mail*, which subsequently ran the play as a serial.[21] It is often speculated that the National Government's victory in a General Election held two weeks later is attributable at least in part to feelings stirred by *Cavalcade*. King George V and Queen Mary even sat in the audience the night of election victory in what was perceived as a gesture of royal gratitude.[22]

Its reputation for jingoism notwithstanding, *Cavalcade*'s dramatic effect is based on a complex orchestration of emotions, particularly those regarding war. As Robert Marryot and Alfred Bridges board the troopship in Act I, the crowd cheers wildly, but Jane, Ellen, and other wives weep bitterly in unresolved emotional counterpoint. In the following scene, the Marryot children play with toy soldiers. Jane asks despairingly if they can't play at any other game but hurting and killing and tells them to go away from her. That Joe does go away from her, to a far greater war than the Boer, is a dramatic irony of considerable impact. In one of the most effective scenes in the play, "1914" appears in lights above the proscenium and slowly fades to "1915," "1916," "1917," "1918," as soldiers are seen marching uphill endlessly, out of darkness and into darkness. Below them a group of brightly dressed and energetic women sing stirring recruiting songs — "Sunday I Walk Out with a Soldier," "We Don't Want to Lose You" — with terrible enthusiasm.

Such discrepancies between the dark realities of war and the bright rhetoric of patriotism cut across distinctions of age, gender, and social class to suggest unresolved issues at the core of our century's emotional history. Jane's New Year toast at the end of the play is a climactic expression of this unresolvedness, for it construes the past and future of England not as a continuity but as a coupling, the glories and sorrows of national life not as balanced but as survived.

As part of the complex orchestration of emotions in the play, the antiwar rhetoric is relieved with moments indulgently sentimental. Jane and Margaret watch a dated music-hall sketch about a princess disguised as a milkmaid, and the sketch treats us to several choruses of "The Mirabelle Waltz" before the stage manager breaks in to announce the relief of Mafeking. Through a black iron fence that seems to represent the protectedness of their world, we watch silent strollers in Kensington Gardens dressed in elaborate mourning for Queen Victoria. In fond commemoration of Victorian excess, their solemn procession includes a dog wearing an enormous crepe bow on his collar. Amiably sentimental — perhaps the finest moment in the play — is a scene in which the

Marryot children watch Victoria's funeral cortege with
no sense of the occasion. Movedly, Jane notes that five
kings ride behind the dead queen and, famously, little
Joe comments that Victoria must have been a very little
lady.

The play's mixture of antiwar invective, patriotic
flag-waving, and sentimentality is a perfectly balanced
formula for capturing the history of thirty tumultuous
years without appearing to have a special point of view.
If the majority of playgoers found *Cavalcade* staunchly
patriotic, others suspected it of tongue-in-cheek patriotism,[23] and at least one reviewer was enraged by
what she perceived as its sentimentalizing of war.[24] The
play offers so many and such varied points of view that
it accommodates almost any understanding. What better way to evoke the period with authenticity for those
who had lived it? History is not a course pursued in
Cavalcade, but a gauntlet run — and run by such flickering illumination that it managed to seem everyone's rite
of passage.

The years have robbed *Cavalcade* of this lived-
through appeal, but the play remains important for its
theatricality. There are dozens of moments in the play
when small bits of stage business and understated grace
notes in the dialogue are as impressively calculated as the
grandly melodramatic effects. When newlywed Edith
says to Edward Marryot that the moment is their own
forever and then takes her cloak from the ship's railing,
disclosing the words "S. S. *Titanic*" on a life preserver,
the scene has a theatrical economy spoiled only by its
having become a cinematic cliché. At the end of sending
Joe off to war while betraying nothing of what she feels,
Jane lights a cigarette for the first time in the play and
in that single, uncharacteristic action, bespeaks elo-
quently the strain of farewell. Just informed of Joe's
death in battle, she joins the Armistice celebration in
Trafalgar Square and with a blank face brandishes a rat-

tle and blows a squeaker. With a consummate sense of
scene, Coward has the crowd melt away and leave Jane
alone in the square, her noisemakers drowned by the full
strength of the orchestra playing "Land of Hope and
Glory." "Not quite psychologically accurate," Coward
noted of the scene, "but undeniably effective."[25]

The final scene of *Cavalcade* carries the emotions
of the play into the present. Set in a night club, that most
typical of 1930s institutions, the scene calls for decora-
tions angular and strange and music discordant in its
harmonies, disenchanted in its sentiment. Famously,
Fanny Bridges sings "Twentieth Century Blues":

> In this strange illusion,
> Chaos and confusion,
> People seem to lose their way.
> What is there to strive for,
> Love or keep alive for?

Gradually a visual coda displaces the nightclub scene:
war casualties wearing hospital uniforms are seen making baskets; Jane and Robert are glimpsed raising their
glasses in a New Year toast; Margaret appears dancing
with a man noticeably younger than she; Ellen sits
before a radio microphone. As such scenes flash quickly
on and off, an illuminated sign spells out contemporary
news in the darkness, and the noise of steam riveters,
loudspeakers, jazz bands, and airplanes overwhelms the
orchestra. Chaos reigns until darkness and silence creep
over the stage. Then the lights slowly come up; the
Union Jack flutters aloft, and the massive cast, arrayed
on tiers, sings "God Save the King" in full voice as the
curtain descends.

The ending is generally regarded today as the most
shameless claptrap, but its cavalier juxtaposition of chaos
and national faith crowns the flickering illuminations of
the play with suitable ambiguity. Are we to understand that faith in king and country can withstand the
"twentieth-century blues?" That such faith triumphs

over chaos? That it simply coexists with despair in some mindless doublethink? John Lahr argues that the last scene carries the play from history through nightmare to prophecy,[26] but such an understanding does not adequately consider either the ingrained ambivalence of the play's mood, Coward's indifference to patriotism until World War II, or the cynicism that lurks in his brazen flag-waving. *Cavalcade* is marvelous spectacle and virtually a five-finger exercise in theater, but as patriotic melodrama it is oddly uncommitted. "I hadn't written the play as a dashing patriotic appeal at all," Coward insisted in his autobiography. "There was certainly love of England in it, a certain natural pride in some of our very typical characteristics, but primarily it was the story of thirty years in the life of a family."[27]

This Happy Breed

This Happy Breed was written in May 1939, as the darkness of World War II was threatening England. It was for all intents and purposes a call to arms—both an insistence that Englishmen be ready to fight for their liberties and a condemnation of Chamberlain's policy of appeasing Germany. Coward had not sought the role of patriot imposed on him by *Cavalcade*, but he had grown into the role by 1939, and his sense of national duty decreed he forge ahead with rehearsals of *This Happy Breed* even though he suspected there was little chance it would see production before the outbreak of hostilities. History proved his misgivings valid: England announced herself at war in September 1939, and Coward disbanded his cast forthwith. By the time the play was produced in London in 1943, it was no longer a call to arms but an ambiguous look backward. Critics were nevertheless enthusiastic—perhaps more enthusiastic than they would have been in politically nervous 1939.

The play begins on the day the Gibbons family moves into 17 Sycamore Road, Clapham Common, and all scenes take place in the family dining room. The homesteaders include Frank Gibbons, a few weeks discharged from the army; his wife Ethel and her mother Mrs. Flint; his sister Sylvia; and his three children, Reg, Queenie, and Vi. To Frank's delight he finds that Bob Mitchell, an army acquaintance, lives in the adjoining house with his wife and son Billy. Sam Leadbitter and Phyllis Blake, friends (later spouses) of Fred and Ethel's children, complete the cast. The play chronicles the lives of these characters between 1919 and 1939. Events like the General Strike of 1926, the abdication of Edward VIII, and Chamberlain's visit to Munich are glimpsed in the background, but the focus is on domestic life during the swift procession of years.

The cast of characters is an ironically unhappy variant of Shakespeare's "happy breed of men." Sylvia and Mrs. Flint quarrel continuously, and Frank and Ethel, though they love each other, are often at odds temperamentally. Under Sam Leadbitter's influence, Reg adopts a Bolshevik posture that vexes his father, and Queenie offends her family deeply by treating them as déclassé. Vi falls in love with Sam Leadbitter but feels she must spurn him because of his unhealthy influence over Reg, and Billy Mitchell falls in love with Queenie, who will not permit herself to return his love until all other possibilities of life are closed to her. Vi and Sam eventually marry but are killed in a car crash a year or two later, and Queenie runs away at one point with a married man, setting her mother against her. Christmas dinner in 1925 finds brothers and sisters quarreling; the General Strike pits generation against generation as well as class against class; and Reg and Phyllis's wedding day is virtually a Donnybrook Fair.

The Gibbonses muddle through these contretemps and tragedies because they have what Frank calls "horse

sense." It is British horse sense, he implies, that makes
political conservatives out of youths who flirt with Bolshevism, that brings Queenie finally to the altar with
Billy, and that keeps him and Ethel together through the
years. Lecturing his infant grandson climactically, Frank
issues the play's call to arms in precisely such terms. The
ordinary people, he says, know better than the politi-
cians what they belong to, where they came from, and
where they are going, and they know these things not
with their brains but with their roots. The ordinary people know, too, that they haven't struggled for hundreds
of years to secure decency and justice and freedom for
themselves without being prepared to fight fifty wars to
retain them.

There can be little question that Coward was at-
tempting in *This Happy Breed* to recapture the patriotic
impact of *Cavalcade*, for both plays employ the formula
of two families demonstrating their mettle as Englishmen while great events unroll in the background over
several decades. The formula is more theatrically effective in *Cavalcade* than in its successor, however. *This
Happy Breed* has not the dazzle of *Cavalcade* — its impressive array of sets, its hundreds of characters on stage,
its thousands of costumes, its full orchestra, its lusty
chorus of "God Save the King." It has not the sustained
tension between the upper and lower classes that invigorates *Cavalcade*. Nor has it anything like *Cavalcade*'s
mime scenes in Kensington Gardens and Trafalgar Square
to enlarge our viewpoint from the domestic to the national. Locked into a single utilitarian set and a single
dramatic mode, *This Happy Breed* is essentially domestic
melodrama.

Even the background events seem smaller in *This
Happy Breed* than in *Cavalcade*. The General Strike is
something of a lark for both Mr. Gibbons and Reg, its
emotional cost not comparable to that of the Boer War
in *Cavalcade*. The resignation of Edward VIII stands as

an effective emblem of change in the Gibbonses' life, but it barely touches the characters' emotional lives and seems unimportant compared to the death of Victoria in the earlier play. World War II looms threateningly for the Gibbonses but not like World War I for the Marryots, inasmuch as the Gibbonses have no son to lose in the war and seem not to worry about their son-in-law in the navy. Reg's death in an automobile accident is only a domestic tragedy and seems dramaturgically mean compared to the deaths of Edward Marryot aboard the *Titanic* and of Joe Marryot in battle on the eve of the 1918 armistice.

There are several reasons why Coward might have chosen to domesticize the formula of *Cavalcade* in this way. Doubtful that *This Happy Breed* would reach production, he would probably have judged multiple sets and a cast of hundreds financially improvident. Knowing that *Cavalcade* was still fondly remembered, he would have wanted to vary its formula so that he would not seem to be repeating himself, and attenuation of the formula was a more reasonable mode of change than amplification. It seems likely, too, that he had grown weary of his reputation as a playboy and wanted to remind London that he knew something about the sort of Englishman who lived in Clapham Common. An introduction to the play he wrote in 1954 suggests a lingering grievance that he was not credited with a working knowledge of such people. "Having been born in Teddington and having lived respectively at Sutton, Battersea Park, and Clapham Common during all my formative years," he wrote, "I can confidently assert that I know a great deal more about the hearts and minds of ordinary South Londoners than [the critics] gave me credit for."[28]

Coward's protestation notwithstanding, the residents of Clapham Common never quite come to life in the play. They fret, they storm, and they turn to one another affectionately, but they never fully engage our interest.

Mrs. Flint's bladder is a matter of some family concern, but her trips to the loo are simply realistic, not the wry divertissements that might be expected. In other plays, Coward found Christian Science a rich source of humor, but Sylvia's conversion to the sect occasions little more than a petulant distaste on Frank's part for her saying that people have "passed over" or "been taken." Reg's innate respect for his father and Frank's fatherly understanding are drearily bromidic, and Queenie's notion that she is an arbiter of taste is merely sad, not the stylistic fun it might have been. The best speech in the play is Mrs. Flint's anecdote about a friend who was doing her shopping at eleven o'clock, putting a roast in the oven at twelve, and at half past one found herself in the hospital lying flat on her back on the operating table. It is significant that Cole Lesley suggested the speech to Coward, for Coward's instinct was to suppress all such lightness in favor of Clapham Common heaviness.[29]

If *This Happy Breed* has been successful in production, it is because Coward's respect for British staunchness survives this heaviness of treatment. Indeed, the play has always struck its audiences as sensationally sober, as almost a recantation of Coward's notorious frivolity. A reviewer in the *Daily Telegraph* congratulated Coward in 1943 upon a "quickening and deepening of the imagination," upon "spiritual growth."[30] On the occasion of a 1956 production on American television, Ward Morehouse congratulated The Master upon overcoming his taste for flippancy and "presenting a deep understanding of the strife and the tears, the strains and the bickering, the joys and the triumphs of his English family."[31]

Such reviewers overshot their rhetorical mark, perhaps, but they rightly understood Coward to be treating serious matters in a more serious way than before. By the late 1930s, Coward was sentimentally a royalist, economically a capitalist, and emotionally divided between worshiping the aristocracy and keeping faith with the middle class. It is not surprising that he came to mistrust any political development that threatened a social order in which he found such latitude. The throb of sincerity in Frank Gibbons's lines is Coward's own endorsement of the status quo, and the general humorlessness of the play suggests that genuine threats to the structure of society were no more amusing to Coward in 1939 than to Frank Gibbons. Reg had once nagged them because they were living on the fat of the land while the poor workers were starving, observes Frank with a shrug, and now they have Queenie turning on them because they are déclassé. In his unemphatic, sobersided way, Frank remains faithful to the middle ground, and Coward makes him function as a magnet, drawing his family back to the middle ground from the extremes of righteousness, Bolshevism, and plutocracy. He also appoints Frank peacemaker in the family, suggesting that peacemaking and the dangerous appeasements of Chamberlain were quite different impulses. With equally felicitous touch, he makes Frank the most loving of the characters, suggesting that a conservative view of class is entirely consonant with fine feelings.

It remains a problem, however, that happy moments are rare in the play, as if staunchness of spirit were not quite compatible with happiness. Although he wanted to honor the middle class for preserving social stability in England, Coward seems not to have been able to repress a discordant sense that life in such places as Clapham Common is death to the spirit. As a result of such warring impulses in the play, unresolved questions about its composition proliferate. Why, one wonders, did Coward entitle the play "This Happy Breed," sardonically emphasizing the unhappiness of his characters? Having decided to affirm the world of Clapham Common, why was he unable to say that it offered more than the pleasures of gardening and grandchildren? Did he mean to imply that not only were wit and sophistication lacking in Clapham Common but that they were necessary to civilized happiness? Having built a career by joking about society's foibles, why did he lose all sense of humor in coming to society's defense? One critic has implied that such questions disappear if we understand the play as an appeal "from above to above, pretending by mimetic means, to come from below," but such an understanding introduces a new problem of unalloyed cynicism.[32] Ultimately, *This Happy Breed* may prove less interesting as melodrama than as a psychodramatic clue to Coward's personal confusions.

Waiting in the Wings

Although it is the most appealing and durable of his postwar plays, *Waiting in the Wings* is evidence of Coward's weakening craftsmanship as he approached his sixth decade of life. The history of his attitude toward the text suggests that weakening. Conceived in April 1958, the play was abandoned a year later, barely two acts written, with the unflinching admission in Coward's diary that "although the characters are good and the dialogue, of course, excellent, there is no play."[33] Inexplicably, the discarded manuscript seemed to him quite fine a year later, and by the middle of April 1960, he had written a third act, had done "a tremendous amount of cutting and snipping and transposing," and had proclaimed *Waiting in the Wings* a "strong, well-constructed play."[34] The critics did not agree with this evaluation when the play opened in London in September, and Coward was furious. In an unusually public show of temper, he denounced his critics to Cecil Wilson of the *Daily Mail* ("Let them reserve their raves for those dreary little experimental plays that only they can understand and nobody goes to see unless he wants to be bored to death")[35] and wrote a series of three articles for the *Sunday Times* condemning the New Wave playwrights his critics seemed to prefer.[36] It was all rather churlish and sad—an unworthy denouement for The Master's fiftieth produced work.

Waiting in the Wings is set literally in "The Wings," a charity home for retired leading ladies. Martha Carrington, whom we never see, is bedridden at the age of ninety-five, and pyromaniac Sarita Myrtle is quite mad, but the other actresses who live in The Wings are simply bored and humiliated by their reduced circumstances. Bonita Belgrave and Cora Clarke are well paired, the former a complainer, the latter a complainer about complainers. May Davenport and Lotta Bainbridge are also well paired—enemies for thirty years over a husband shared seriatim, finally friends in Act III. Deirdre O'Malley stands apart from the other residents not only for her Irish brogue but for her tendency to see life melodramatically, as if The Wings were set in *East Lynne*. Sylvia Archibald, known as "Miss Archie," is superintendent of the home, and Perry Lascoe is secretary to its governing board. Both are devoted to the old ladies, for Miss Archie has not outgrown her years as an ENSA colonel, and Perry is unabashedly in love with actresses.

The play follows no coherent line of action. It begins with Lotta's entrance into the home, and among its intermittent concerns are the proposed building of a solarium, May's running quarrel with Lotta, Sarita's playing with matches, and the visit of an unscrupulous reporter named Zelda Fenwick, to whom Perry unwisely grants an interview. Each of these concerns is brought dutifully to climax: the solarium is finally built with money provided by Zelda's publisher; May abruptly ends her quarrel with Lotta; Sarita sets fire to her bedroom and very nearly to the house; and Perry is dismissed by the board for allowing Zelda access to The Wings, then rehired. Further complicating life in The Wings is the

unexpected death of Deirdre on Christmas night and the
appearance of Lotta's son Alan to rescue his mother from
penury after thirty-three years of alienation. Lotta is not
disposed to be rescued, however, and the play ends as
it began, with the entrance of a new resident and the
ladies setting out to make her feel welcome.

Coward's passions probably ran high over the critical rejection of *Waiting in the Wings* because the play
brought together three important strains of his consciousness — a sensitivity to encroaching old age and its horrors
for the improvident, an abiding fondness for elderly actresses, and an awareness of institutional homes based
on his having served for twenty years as a very active
president of the Actors' Orphanage. The general sentimentality of the play is perhaps due also to the conflu-
ence of these emotionally-laden awarenesses.

Lotta carries the burden of the play's sentimentality. She is independent, reconciled to her circumstances,
and unfailingly gracious — very much a grande dame.
Her stiff upper lip is tremulous at the end of the first
scene when her former maid leaves her to the uncertain
mercies of the home, but her poise is sentimentally effective largely because it seems to enshroud despair. At
the end of the second scene in Act I, she observes that
there is little time left and adds a quiet, "Thank God."
A maid's announcement of her son's surprise visit prompts
a sudden hand to her throat, briefly closed eyes, and then
a brave command to let him come in. That she refuses
Alan's offer of a home is a gesture as proud and wise as
it is predictable. Indeed, the entire development with
Alan seems to have no dramatic function other than to
wrench Lotta's emotions.

Even more sentimentally rendered than Lotta is
Osgood Meeker, a septuagenarian who brings violets regularly to Martha Carrington, now in her dotage, just as
he brought them years before to her stage door. Zelda
belittles his attachment, but Osgood's starstruck sweet-

ness triumphs over journalistic cynicism. To Zelda's observation that Martha hadn't much of a voice, he answers that she probably hadn't much of anything, really, except magic. Martha is not dying upstairs, he corrects Zelda, but *living* upstairs, and she will never fully die, he thinks, "not quite."

The play offers any number of such moments. May's heroic intercession to save Perry's job is sentimentally affecting, if implausible, and Zelda's appearance at the home on Christmas night with a case of champagne is an atonement for her exploitation of the residents that offers a fine opportunity for emotional display. Unsentimental Deirdre, obsessed with misery, the imminence of death, and her Irish heritage, dies while dancing an Irish jig; and with accomplished, curtain-line sentimentality, May comments, "The luck of the Irish."

Waiting in the Wings would be unbearably sentimental were it only a sequence of such moments, but relieving the sentimental and lending it point is a nice candor about age and its problems. Finishing a game of canasta with Bonita, Cora suggests they hold off settling accounts until the next time they play. Bonita says she thought Cora would say that, and to Cora's imperious demand to know why she should think such a thing, Bonita answers longsufferingly that it is what she always says. Deirdre is venomous about the malfunctioning of a television set, but it breaks down only when she assaults it with her cane. Perry observes bromidically that the elderly can recall something like Queen Victoria's Jubilee but not be able to remember what happened the previous week. From the viewpoint of life in the home, Cora responds acidicly, "Nothing did." In her loonier moments, Sarita likes to declaim Shakespeare. She must *not* quote *Macbeth* in The Wings, Miss Archie rebukes her, knowing too well, we imagine, that Macbeth's soliloquies discompose those residents who do not accept death as their lot.

The residents' professional skills add greatly to the liveliness of dialogue and situation. An actress named Dolly Drexell is remembered with professional bitchiness for china blue eyes and no middle register. The infamous Boodie Nethersole, an actress who sits on the board of governors, is deemed unable to act her way out of a paperbag. Maud congratulates herself on stopping the show *Miss Mouse* with her singing, and Cora remarks too expertly that it was the notices that really stopped the show. Upstaging and timing are arts in which the ladies continually exercise themselves. Bonita remarks feelingly upon Osgood's devotion to Martha, and May quotes Shakespeare to good effect: "Love alters not with his brief hours and weeks / But bears it out even to the edge of doom." Deirdre, who is often accused of harping on death, wants to know who is harping on death now, and May answers briskly, "William Shakespeare." "I might have known it," says Deirdre with a snort. "An unlikely contingency," says May.

A cast composed almost entirely of such leading ladies is quintessentially a camp idea, but Coward plays the idea for sentiment on the whole rather than for archness. Sarita is the notable exception. It is a part of her madness to fancy herself always on stage and ever the leading lady. Making small talk, Zelda asks her if The Wings isn't a very nice house, and Sarita answers blithely, "Capacity." Almost nothing distracts her from a leading lady's concerns. She is happy at The Wings, she says, except on matinée days, when she finds the tea trays distracting. And the people are kind to her, she confesses — sometimes a little dull in the first act, but generally keen by the second act. Rushed from her burning bedroom in a blanket, she enquires why she is wearing such a strange garment: "Is it to be an oriental production?" Departing The Wings at the end of Act II for an asylum that can better handle her pyromania, she bids adieu to the assembled residents with the graciousness proper to her imagined status and thanks them for a really lovely engagement.

Sarita's mad graciousness is an echo of Lotta's grande dame manner, but it functions less as parody than as thematic reinforcement. The integrity of her mad role points up Lotta's integrity and the psychological strain of its maintenance, just as Cora and Bonita's inconsequential war of words points up the inconsequence of May and Lotta's thirty-year feud. The parodic element is present in both parallels, keeping sentimentality and melodrama in bounds, but theatricality is the more deeply shared note. Sarita's role-playing even makes us wonder if Lotta's sincerity is not the self-deluding sincerity of a great actress.

The special delight of *Waiting in the Wings* is this off-balancing of sentiment with the possibility of theatrical illusion — which amounts, perhaps, to an off-balancing of Coward's heartfelt feeling for elderly actresses with the cynicism born of his experience.[37] When Cora enters from the new solarium in the last scene crying that she can't bear to sit under its "ghastly glass" another minute, she reverses her earlier enthusiasm for the solarium not only querulously but dramatically, with a thoroughly professional sense of effect. Just so, there is a professional edge to Lotta's choice of a role opposite May. Her ostensible acceptance of life in The Wings plays well against May's unacceptance, and her public wish to mend the quarrel plays effectively against May's unforgivingness.

This edging of sentiment with the cynicism of the theatrically adept does not redeem the shapelessness of plot in *Waiting in the Wings*, but, like the candor about old age and its problems, it does much to relieve the play's overflowing measure of sentiment. In the final scene, Coward brings sentiment and cynicism together nicely. Topsy Baskerville, who replaces Sarita as a resident, enters to a carefully staged effect — the assembled troupers welcoming her with a performance of her signature tune. That there is genuine sympathy for her at that difficult moment of her life and that the residents' sympathy is not belied by their stagy contrivance are Coward's final tributes of respect and affection to his leading ladies, but they are his reminder, too, that actresses are professional orchestrators of emotion.

A Song at Twilight

In 1966 Coward appeared for the last time on a West End stage, in a trilogy of plays called *Suite in Three Keys* that he had written for himself. The trilogy is made up of *A Song at Twilight*, the longest and best play of the three; *Shadows of the Evening*, a one-act, one-note melodrama about confronting death; and *Come into the Garden Maud*, a comedy in two scenes whose best joke was Coward's casting himself as a plainspoken American. Performed in alternate repertoire, the plays were the fulfillment of Coward's desire to round off his career with "a sort of acting orgy swan-song."[38] He thought it a particular triumph of craftsmanship that the three plays used the same set — a hotel suite in Switzerland — and that the cast of each play required only three characters and a waiter named Felix.[39] The plays are as modest in their achievement as in their requirements, but Coward had become a Grand Old Man of the Theater by 1966, and reviewers were enthusiastic. Peter Lewis, writing in the *Daily Mail*, expressed the general approbation: "As the curtain fell last night I felt oddly elated, as if I had recaptured the flavour of an elusive drink that one tasted when young but which had never been mixed quite right since. I know the name of it . . . not mannerism, not bravura, not histrionics, but style."[40]

The central character of *A Song at Twilight* is Hugo Latymer, an elderly writer of considerable eminence,

whose sole concern has become the polishing and pro-
tecting of his reputation. To this end, he refuses to allow
his novels to be filmed, insists upon due reverence from
all around him, and refuses to acknowledge he is homosexual, even in a decade of sexual tolerance. His wife
Hilde, who functions primarily as his secretary, has long
since guessed the truth about his sexuality, but the subject does not arise between them until an actress named
Carlotta Gray asks permission to quote in her memoirs
from the love letters she had received from Hugo many
years before. With typical arrogance, Hugo refuses, insisting in Shaw's words to Mrs. Patrick Campbell that
he has no intention of playing the horse to her Lady
Godiva. Piqued, Carlotta answers that she will return
the letters he wrote to her, but not his letters to Perry
Sheldon. What does she know about Perry Sheldon, Hugo
demands. Among other things, she knows that Sheldon
was the true love of Hugo's life.

In the second act, Carlotta makes it clear that she
is offended not by Hugo's homosexuality but by his cruelty and moral cowardice, which she finds especially evident in his public labeling of the deceased Perry Sheldon
as only an "adequate secretary." Implying that she might
give the letters in her possession to a scholar researching
Hugo's life, she proposes a moment of truth and an act
of repentance. The great writer refuses to unbend, and
it is left to Hilde to insist that Sheldon was not worth the
passions they are expending on his behalf. He was a
foolish, conceited, dishonest, and self-indulgent man, she
insists. Abruptly, Carlotta has a change of heart and
hands Hugo the compromising letters. In return, he
grants her permission to publish his ostensibly heterosexual love letters. The curtain descends as Hugo reads
his letters to Sheldon with evident emotion.

The best moments in this minor play are exchanges
in which Coward's dialogue works its old alchemy, trans-
forming social irritation into verbal champagne. Hugo

demands imperiously to know what Carlotta wants of him, and she answers insouciantly that at the moment, she wants only dinner. Owing to its careful nurturing, his "bubble reputation" has the solidity of a football, she snaps in a later exchange, so he shouldn't be surprised if people kick it about a bit. Interestingly, but as if he no longer trusted his dialogue to justify the states of mind that prompt it, Coward even defends his penchant for scenes of irritation. Carlotta warns Hugo not to minimize the power of that apparently trivial emotion — that irritation can be more powerful than anger and more destructive than hatred. It can also wreak havoc with the gentlest of dispositions, she says. She might be speaking of the comic technique in any one of Coward's plays.

But the weaknesses of A Song at Twilight tend to eclipse such luminous moments. Carlotta's possession of Perry Sheldon's letters is too coincidental, and Hilde's condemnation of Perry Sheldon is unrealistically knowledgeable. The changes of heart at the final curtain are inadequately motivated, just as the relationship between Hilde and Carlotta is insufficiently worked. Most debilitating of all, perhaps, a general ineffectiveness of speech betrays the flagging energy of Coward's imagination. When Hugo admits that he once had homosexual tendencies, Coward has Carlotta respond, "Homosexual tendencies in the past! What nonsense! You've been a homosexual all your life, and you know it!" Charles Kindl's more vigorous rendering of the speech for a shortened version of the play illumines the flatness of Coward's original lines: "Tendencies in the past! What nonsense! You're as queer as a coot and have been all your life."[41]

A Song at Twilight is of especial interest because it is the only one of Coward's plays to deal importantly with a homosexual character. Coward never attempted to conceal his own homosexuality from friends, but he resembled Hugo Latymer in making public show of friendships with women and in feeling that his career

necessitated sexual discretion. Because of these correspondences, it has been widely assumed that *A Song at
Twilight* is autobiographical and that Coward was dealing candidly with a subject he had previously approached
only metaphorically, as in Nicky Lancaster's drug addiction in *The Vortex*, or veiledly, as in the frivolity of
young men like Simon Bliss in *Hay Fever*, or inversely,
as in speciously heterosexual songs like "Mad About the
Boy" and "Matelot."

It is possibly the case that Hugo's dilemma was
Coward's nightmare fantasy, but there is no other autobiographical resonance. Coward had neither impulse
nor cause to accuse himself of Hugo's nastiness, and the
circumstances of his private life in no way resembled
those of Hugo. The model for Hugo was in fact Somerset
Maugham, whose crustiness in old age was so like Hugo's
that Maugham's nephew nearly fainted when he read a
draft of the play and recognized his uncle — or so The
Master reported.[42] And the situation in which Hugo
finds himself was inspired not by anything in Coward's
life but by an incident between Max Beerbohm and
Constance Collier, which Coward read about in David
Cecil's biography of Beerbohm.[43]

The homosexual interest of *A Song at Twilight* is most
striking for Coward's ambivalence toward Hugo. The
character is on the one hand a type of homosexual that
Coward disliked, and he scorns Hugo for marrying, for
denying his inclination in private, and for slighting a
man who was once his lover. On the other hand, Hugo
is pathetic, as Maugham was pathetic in his dotage, and
Coward allows this unpleasant man to keep his secret at
the end and to respond with uncharacteristic graciousness to Carlotta's surrender of the letters. In short, the
portrait is more black-white than the gray we might expect. Equally irresolute is Coward's refusal to let Hugo
speak out in defense of his sexual orientation. There is
homosexual advocacy in the play, to be sure — made po-

tent by the fact that Parliament was rewriting the laws governing homosexual acts concurrently with the run of the play — but it is heterosexual Carlotta and not homosexual Hugo who is Coward's advocate of tolerance.

A Song at Twilight is, in the last analysis, a curious theatrical contrivance: Coward playing an unattractive homosexual while speaking out for the legalization of homosexual acts through the voice of a heterosexual woman. The contrivance is perhaps no more than the flirtation with public disclosure that Coward practiced all his professional life, but one must be impressed with its concealments. Apparently, the freedoms of the 1960s were no more than interesting to a homosexual who had practiced the arts of obfuscation for a half-century of public-life.

5

~~~~~~

The Revues, Operettas,
and Songs

In the decade following World War I, the most successful musical entertainments were revues — capacious
amalgams of specialty acts, production numbers, and
skits, whose brisk presentation seems to have suited the
postwar mood. Many of the 1920s revues were tawdry
affairs, depending for their appeal upon slapstick comedy and an abundance of female flesh, but the impre-
sarios André Charlot and C. B. Cochran insisted on
production values that made their revues the most acclaimed in London. Coward was delighted, therefore,
when Charlot commissioned him to write the lyrics and
music for the revue *London Calling!* (1923) and to col-
laborate with Ronald Jeans on its book. Critics applauded
the finished product, especially the haunting ballad
"Parisian Pierrot" and the song "What Love Means to
Girls Like Me." A burlesque of the Sitwells entitled "The
Swiss Family Whittlebot" earned some of the first ac-
colades of record for Coward's wit.

The success of *London Calling!* established Coward's career as a librettist, but it was several years before
he was trusted with artistic responsibility for all facets
of a revue. C. B. Cochran commissioned him to write
the book and lyrics for a 1925 revue called *On with the
Dance* but refused to allow him sole responsibility for the
music. Although piqued by Cochran's caution, Coward
threw himself into preparations for the show with an

energy that became the revue's distinctive note. "At times the players seemed mad," wrote one reviewer, "intoxicated with the desire to force their bodies to do something faster, faster."[1] Greatly admired were "Poor Little Rich Girl," the hit song of the show, and a sketch entitled "Oranges and Lemons," in which two male actors portray elderly ladies undressing and getting into a strange bed together in a rooming house.

After *London Calling!*, Coward and Cochran enjoyed a working relationship for nine years, during which time Coward wrote and Cochran produced the revues *This Year of Grace!* (1928) and *Words and Music* (1932), the operettas *Bitter Sweet* (1929) and *Conversation Piece* (1934), and the panoramic spectacle *Cavalcade*. *This Year of Grace!* is the finest of Coward's revues — witty, graceful, melodic, distinguished for such favorite Coward songs as "A Room with a View," "Dance Little Lady," and "World Weary."[2] His sketches were never more finely drawn than "The Bus Rush," an inspired bit of nonsense that mocks the English penchant for queuing, and "The English Lido Beach," with its unhappily rusticating vacationers. Nor is Coward's talent for the ingenuous stage device anywhere more evident than in "A Tube Station," a musical sketch in which a whistling urchin infects first one, than another stolid Londoner, until the whole crowd gathered at a tube station breaks out in an exuberant dance. St. John Ervine, writing in the *Observer*, called the revue "the most amusing, the most brilliant, the cleverest, the daintiest, the most exquisite, the most fanciful, the most graceful, the happiest. . . ."[3] Superlatives finally failed him.

Words and Music is nearly as estimable a revue as *London Calling!* The song "Let's Say Good-Bye" has a wry charm that has survived its voguish understatement, and such drolly comic songs as "Mad Dogs and Englishmen," "Housemaids' Knees," and "The Wife of an Acrobat" remain favorites today. A travesty of R. C. Sherriff's

play *Journey's End* as it might have been produced by
Erik Charell is wonderfully improbable, as is "Midnight
Matinée," an historical pageant produced by titled and
nouveau riche ladies, whose amateur staging runs giddily
amok.

Sigh No More (1945), the last of Coward's revues,
was disparaged by its creator: the title, he quipped,
"turned out to be the best part."[4] London audiences,
however, found The Master's talent for acidic wit and
wisdom undiminished. They delighted in a sketch he
wrote for Joyce Grenfell disproving its thesis that "Trav-
elling Broadens the Mind," and the songs "Nina" and "I
Wonder What Happended to Him" became instant favorites, the first about an Argentine lady who "resolutely
wouldn't dance," the second about officers and gentlemen immured in the Indian Army and insatiably given
to gossip. The weakness of *Sigh No More* is its hodge-
podge assembly. Justifiably, the *Times* observed that it
was "without the impress of a definite style — disconcert-
ingly, because it has been 'written, composed, and directed' by Mr. Noel Coward."[5]

With the revue so much in his blood, Coward
tended to treat the straightforward musical play as a variety show overlaid with story line. He was aware that
the so-called "book" musical had become a theatrical
ideal in the wake of *Showboat*, but he found difficulty
in accommodating the new standards of libretto-score
integration and wholeness of style. A plot device was
usually his inspiration for a musical, but he would then
write songs that required precise situations, and the situations would be dropped into the plot like firecrackers
into a pudding. Surprisingly, perhaps, Coward did not
give the same attention to dialogue in his musical plays
as in his straight comedies. Dialogue remained for him
what it was in the musical sketch — introduction, bridge,
and patch. As a consequence, his musicals tend to struc-
tural creakiness and to defy attempts today at revival.

Among Coward's musical plays, *Bitter Sweet* has proved most durable. A romantic operetta in the nostalgic, *Fledermaus* tradition, it traces the career of the Marchioness of Shayne from her elopement as a young woman, to her employment in a Viennese café, to the death of her husband at the hands of a lecherous military officer, to her operatic successes, to her second, aristocratic marriage — all as background for her efforts in old age to persuade a young woman to elope with a jazz pianist. The rousing military chorus "Tokay," the lovely waltz "I'll See You Again," and a send-up of 1890s aestheticism entitled "Green Carnation" give distinction to a melodious score, and the patchiness of the book seems consistent with the Viennese mode, almost a pleasantry of the genre. The Viennese formula is less successful in *Conversation Piece*, an operetta that traces the efforts of a duke-turned-adventurer to pass off a young singer as his ward in Regency Brighton. But *Conversation Piece* has some of *Bitter Sweet*'s period charm and a fine theme song, "I'll Follow My Secret Heart," to recommend it.

None of Coward's musicals had the stage success of his revues. *Pacific 1860* (1946), *Ace of Clubs* (1950), *After the Ball* (1954), *Sail Away* (1961), and *The Girl Who Came to Supper* (with Harry Kurnitz, 1963) were all clunkers with wonderful moments, memorable now for isolated songs they included and sometimes excluded — songs like "Nothing Can Last for Ever" and "Chase Me, Charlie" from *Ace of Clubs*, and songs like "Uncle Harry" and "Bronxville Darby and Joan," dropped from *Pacific 1860* and *Sail Away*.[6] All of these musicals misfired primarily because of underworked books, a peculiar failing for a writer who had demonstrated so often that the thinnest material was adequate for his art. Coward was so instinctive a master of the airy construct, it would seem, that when he felt no imperative to spin golden threads in a vacuum, he could not properly draw upon his resources. One suspects that he never really accepted the aesthetic of the book musical or understood how fundamentally that aesthetic had changed musical theater.

Coward wanted to be remembered for his plays, but he is best known today for his songs. He claimed that the songs were a spontaneous flowering of his sensibility, born of an innate fondness for word play and of rhythms and rhymes knocking about in his head. "There is no time I can remember," he once wrote, "when I was not fascinated by words 'going together': Lewis Carroll, Edward Lear, Beatrix Potter, all fed my childish passion, in addition to all the usual nursery rhymes. . . . I can still distinctly recall being exasperated when any of these whimsical effusions were slipshod in rhyming or scansion."[7] He wrote verse all his life but acknowledged that true poetic talent had been denied him.[8] His talent, he recognized, was for doggerel: its tumbling and broken meters, its rough heavy-footedness, its insistent rhymes. Doggerel was suited, he found, to the flippancy that he cultivated as a trademark, and he employed it even in his personal correspondence. "Now sweet Lornie close your eyes / For a wonderful surprise," he once wrote his secretary. "Close your eyes and cross your feet / For a fast approaching treat, / MASTER IN A DAY OR TWO / WILL BE COMING BACK TO YOU!"[9]

Developed as song lyrics and pointed with melody, Coward's doggerel is often brilliantly effective — not the inferior poetry that doggerel is generally thought, but mock poetry that greets sentimentality with a wry, defensive smile. Indeed, Coward is the only English lyricist of his generation who can be named in the same breath with his American contemporaries Cole Porter and Lorenz Hart. Such songs of tempered desire as "If Love Were All" and "Later Than Spring" might have been written by Porter, so delicate is their interplay between sentiment and sentiment overcome, and such impertinent rhymes as "movies" / "prove is" and "phrases" /

"mayonnaise is" might have been devised by Hart in his effort to break with clichés of "June," "moon," and "tune." Coward's lyrics can also bear comparison with those of W. S. Gilbert. Such songs as "His Excellency Regrets" and "I Wonder What Happened to Him" owe a debt to Gilbert's inspired lunacy about servants of the Empire, and choruses in *This Year of Grace!* echo the sweetly credulous, aggressively antiphonal choruses of Gilbert and Sullivan libretti:

CHORUS: Just think of that,
Just think of that,
She got her inspiration at
A patriotic meeting.
Oh, tell us more,
Oh, tell us more,
Oh, tell us what you do it for,
It must be overheating.

DAISY: Kind friends, I thank you all again
And since you ask me to
I will explain.
Like other chaste stenographers
I simply hate photographers,
I also hate publicity.

CHORUS: She lives for sheer simplicity.
("Britannia Rules the Waves")[10]

These parallels notwithstanding, Coward's range as a songwriter places him beyond all meaningful considerations of influence. He could write with macabre glee about "Bad Times Just around the Corner" and with mocking indulgence about "The Stately Homes of England, / How beautiful they stand, / To prove the upper classes / Have still the upper hand." He could write lilting ballads for the operatic voice, as in the scores for *Bitter Sweet* and *After the Ball*, and he could write patter songs that require a tongue as hammeringly true as a typewriter, as in "Mad Dogs and Englishmen." In one temper he could write with grace about "London Pride,"

both the flower and the spirit; in another, he could indulge a taste formed in the music halls of Edwardian
London and write the melodically overripe "Chase Me,
Charlie." His lyrics make a stronger bid for attention
than his melodies, but few effects of the musical theater
were beyond his ability.

Rhyming is central to the art of Coward's lyrics. He
was particularly fond of triple and quadruple rhyme,
and he would make the patness of such rhymes serve as
counterweight for flights of syntactical preciousness.
"What explains this mass mania / To leave Pennsylvania?" he inquires in "Why Do the Wrong People Travel?"
A series of polysyllabic rhymes can be boisterously comic,
as when a chorus sings in *Bitter Sweet*:

> We are the most effectual
> Intellectual
> Movement of the day
> Our moral standards sway
> Like Mrs Tanquerey
> And we are theoretically
> Most aesthetically
> Eager to display
> The fact that we're aggressively
> And excessively
> Anxious to destroy
> All the snobbery
> And hob-nobbery
> Of the hoi-polloi.
> ("Tarara Boom-De-Ay")

Such an intense sequence of rhymes can also function as
characterization. Señorita Nina from Argentina is driven
to frenzy by the beguine tempo, and her too-insistent
rhyming expresses her irritation:

> She said I hate to be pedantic
> But it drives me nearly frantic
> When I see that unromantic
> Sycophantic

> Lot of sluts
> For ever wriggling their guts,
> It drives me absolutely nuts!
> > ("Nina")

In "He Never Did That to Me," a young lady enamored of a movie star sings "I once saw him fish / The Sisters Gish / From out of a stormy sea." The comic effect of the lines derives partly from a rhyme-forced inversion of the normal adjective-noun sequence, partly from the Gish name. Rhymes that invoke the names of celebrities are always humorous in a Coward song, for they jostle reality in the service of an effect absurdly opportune:

> Mr Irving Berlin
> Often emphasizes sin.
> > ("Let's Do It")

> Let's fly away
> Before they send us any more girls
> Like those ubiquitous Gabor girls.
> > ("Let's Fly Away")

> She declined to begin the Beguine
> Though they besought her to
> And in language profane and obscene
> She cursed the man who taught her to,
> She cursed Cole Porter too!
> > ("Nina")

Syncopation is a device Coward used particularly well. He liked to climax a tripping meter and a serpentine scheme of rhymes with the sudden syncopation of a short, thickly accented line:

> Our tastes are very far from Oriental,
> We have a very fixed idea of fun,
> The thought of anything experimental
> We shun.
> We take to innovations very badly,

We'd rather be uncomfortable than not,
In fighting any new suggestion madly
We'd gladly
Be shot!

("English Lido")

As an addendum to a cliché, syncopated lines open the lyric to a sense of cliché overcome:

Women at the tables,
Loosening their sables,
Look at me with cruel eyes,
Then a little something in me dies
And cries.

("I'm So Weary of It All")

In mock servitude to idiom, Coward also liked to open up a meter suddenly and unexpectedly:

In Bengal
To move at all
Is seldom, if ever done.

("Mad Dogs and Englishmen")

Indeed, it is the play of heavily rhymed and metered language against the tyranny of idiom and cliché that usually renders Coward's songs so spirited. His genius was to force a formal structure to accommodate adjectival overloads, elaborate circumlocutions, moralistic interjections, and overly explicit, gossipy detail. It was his conceit that speech is too wayward for such containment and will break out in delicious indiscretions:

Pretty Mrs Bowles
Having had five sausage rolls
Was compelled to leave
      the ball room at a bound
Also Colonel Blake,
Rather gay on tipsy cake,
Emitted first a hiccup
      then a more peculiar sound.

> We can't say what the Vicar did,
> God forbid,
> But we can blame the moonlight
>   and the Spring. . . .
>   ("The Party's Going with a Swing")

Our pleasure in this passage begins with the incongruity of detail: Mrs. Bowles's prettiness, gluttony, and bouncing exit, counterpointed by the ludicrous congruity of "ball" and "bound." It builds climactically as Colonel Blake progresses from tipsiness to hiccups, and thereupon to a flatulence coyly unnamed but wickedly hinted. It culminates with the open beats after "what the Vicar did" and the dead stop to which the rhetorical structure comes and does not come after the injunction "God forbid." These anarchic energies of the doggerel are funnier for Coward's pretense of controlling them with the strong rhymes reinforcing syntax and rhetoric.

The catalogue was Coward's most congenial form because it is amenable to this anarchic interaction of form and content. A song about the Tower of Babel inspired him to a lockstep of rhyme barely able to contain his referential sweep; anapests help to create an impression that the lines are runaway, eager to burst free of the rhymes that rein them in:

> The Chinks and the Japs
> And the Finns and the Lapps
> Were reduced to a helpless stammer,
> And the ancient Greeks
> Took at least six weeks
> To learn their Latin grammar.
> The guttural wheeze
> Of the Portuguese
> Filled the brains of the Danes
> With horror,
> And verbs, not lust,
> Caused the final bust
> In Sodom and Gomorrah.
>   ("Useless Useful Phrases")

In reworking the lyrics to Cole Porter's "Let's Do It," Coward achieved much the same effect. The wealth of indelicate allusions crammed into a highly restricted form suggests that still more material has been suppressed under the discipline of Porter's hobbling rhyme:

> Our leading writers in swarms do it,
> Somerset and all the Maughams do it,
> Let's do it, let's fall in love.
> The Brontës felt that they must do it,
> Mrs Humphry Ward could just do it,
> Let's do it, let's fall in love.
> Anouilh and Sartre — God knows why — do it,
> As a sort of curse
> Eliot and Fry do it,
> But they do it in verse.
> Some mystics as a routine do it,
> Even Evelyn Waugh and Graham Greene do it,
> Let's do it, let's fall in love.
>
> ("Let's Do It")

But for all his skill with rhythmical and rhyming effects, Coward's greater talent was for phrasing — for the unexpected adjective or adverb that invigorates an otherwise homely observation and for the extravagant verb that elevates doggerel to something archly splendid. In "Church Parade," he describes a gaggle of clergymen as looking "quite *aggressively* devout." "Something in a maiden aunt," he quips elsewhere, "just *stupefies* the mind." A bucolic mood leads to the desire for "a horse and plough / Chickens too / Just one cow / With a *wistful* moo." [Emphasis mine] "If you have any mind at all," he assures us solemnly, Gibbon's *Decline and Fall* is "divine," "flimsy," "no more than a whimsy." Mr. Cochran's Young Ladies raised their skirts in 1932 and invited us "to gaze at / Skittish, / Ab-so-lute-ly *Brit*-ish, / Housemaids' knees."

Things British were Coward's best comic subject. "The Stately Homes of England" inspired him to perfectly pitched phrases: the "sporting prints of Aunt Florence's, / Some of which were rather rude," the "very peculiar fowling-piece / Which was sent to Cromwell's niece," the "beastly Roman bowmen" who "bitched our local Yeomen." Most memorably of all, perhaps,

> There's the ghost of a crazy younger son
> Who murdered, in thirteen fifty-one
> An extremely rowdy Nun
> Who resented it.

One delights in the irregular flow of specifics: the over-elaborated date and detailed sonship versus the incredible, quite unexplained rowdiness of the nun. That she *resented* her murder is a triumph of understatement, given force by the shortening of the line.

The insularity of the British people was Coward's special delight. He adored the notions of formal dress worn in the rain forest, of wars won on the playing fields of Eton, and of the sun never setting on Government House, even though such clichés belong more to apocrypha than to history. Englishmen who make no concession to tropical heat are the delightful subject of "Mad Dogs and Englishmen," as crisp of lyric as Coward ever wrote:

> In the Philippines
> There are lovely screens
> To protect you from the glare.
> In the Malay States
> There are hats like plates
> Which the Britishers won't wear.
> At twelve noon
> The natives swoon
> And no further work is done.
> But mad dogs and Englishmen
> Go out in the midday sun.

Coward's Englishmen are even funnier when they break out of their insularity. "People's behaviour / Away from Belgravia, / Would make you aghast," he warns.

The eponymous Uncle Harry, "hotly pursued by dear
Aunt Mary," sets up as a missionary on a South Sea
Island only to discover that the hedonism of the natives
confounds his high sense of purpose. The fall of that good
man is drolly inevitable: "They didn't brandish knives
at him, they really were awfully sweet, / They made
concerted dives at him and offered him things to eat, /
But when they threw their wives at him he had to admit defeat." We are assured in the bouncing refrain
that "Uncle Harry's not a missionary now."

The nemesis of every English citizen traveling abroad
is the realization that Life Is for Living. Mrs. Wentworth-Brewster, exuberantly widowed, is vacationing on
Capri when Life calls to her in a bar on the Piccola
Marina. To cries of "Viva Via che bell' Inglesi" (alter-
nately, "Whoops-adaisy!"), she discovers what the hot-
blooded races have always known:

> Just for fun three young
>   sailors from Messina
> Bowed low to Mrs Wentworth-Brewster,
> Said "Scusi" and politely goosed her.
> Then there was quite a scena.
> Her family, in floods of tears, cried,
> "Leave these men, Mama."
> She said, "They're just high-spirited,
>   like all Italians are
> And most of them have a great deal more
>   to offer than Papa
> In a bar on the Piccola Marina."

Englishmen run to seed in the Raj are male equiva-
lents of Mrs. Wentworth-Brewster. In "I Wonder What
Happened to Him," military gossip goads Coward to
archly British burlesque:

> Whatever became of old Shelley?
> Is it true that young Briggs was cashiered
> For riding quite nude
>   on a push-bike through Delhi

The day the new Viceroy appeared?
Have you had any word
Of that bloke in the "Third,"
Was it Southerby, Sedgewick or Sim?
They had him thrown out of the club
      in Bombay
For, apart from his mess bills
      exceeding his pay,
He took to pig-sticking in *quite*
      the wrong way.
I wonder what happened to him!

In Coward's comic vision, members of royalty are so thoroughly circumscribed by ritual and tradition that he has no need to send them abroad. Hobnobbing at home with the lower orders is lese majesty enough:

Royal condescension
May murmur a Christian Name
But you'll notice a certain tension
If you try to do the same.
                         ("Sir or Ma'am")

And aristocratic children who betray their rank can be as entirely shattering as immorality in the tropics:

Imagine the Duchess's feelings,
You could have pierced her with swords
When she discovered her pet lamb liked Lenin
And sold the *Daily Worker* near the House of Lords.
Her eldest son went to Boodle's and White's
Her second son joined the Blues his father led,
But imagine the Duchess's feelings
When her youngest son went Red!
                    ("Imagine the Duchess's Feelings")

In all these songs that mock English insularity, Coward was more jokester than wasp. His galumphing lords and unhappy duchesses were taken less from life than from the stage, upon which Lord Elderley and Lord Camp had cavorted under various names for decades. Indeed, Coward's satire has always appealed to its purported victims precisely because he limited himself to stock theatrical caricature.

Coward's sentimental songs are less celebrated than his humorous songs, but they have often been found moving, especially in the context of his plays and revues. The best of them are touched with poetry. In *Shadow Play*, a woman remembers the complacency of being young and in love, and her recollection makes admirable use of personification:

> Then, love was complete for us,
> Then, the days were sweet for us,
> Life rose to its feet for us
> And stepped aside
> Before our pride.
>
> ("Then")

"London Pride" catches the sentimental Coward at his best:

> Grey city
> Stubbornly implanted,
> Taken so for granted
> For a thousand years.
> Stay, city,
> Smokily enchanted,
> Cradle of our memories and hopes and fears.

Grayness and smoke ground the emotion in urban reality, but vision transcends such empirical meanness. Beleaguered London is a "cradle" inappositely ancient, dirty but "enchanted," stubborn in its grip but implored to survive the German bombing, "Every Blitz / . . . resistance / Toughening." Like many writers of his generation, Coward thought sentiment had to be hedged with irony if it were to escape sentimentality.

An awareness of time passing or passed is Coward's usual hedge against sentimentality. "Where have they gone — words that rang so true / When Love in our hearts

was new?" he asks in *Operette*, and Parisian Pierrot
knows he is only "The Lord of a day." In *Words and
Music*, daughters who look forward to love cry to their
mother, "Teach us to understand this magic flame, / As
you did when at first your lover came, / What did he
bring to you? / What melodies did he sing to you?" Their
mother answers with a dispassion appropriate to her
years:

> The same . . .
> Melodies that lovers sing
> Whenever the heart is gay with Spring
> And Youth is there.
> I assure you the truth is there.
>   ("The Younger Generation")

The mother's prosaism represents another kind of hedge
against sentimentality in Coward's love songs. It corresponds as a technique to the off-handed cynicism of
"Let's Say Good-Bye":

> Let's look on love as a plaything.
> All these sweet moments we've known
> Mustn't be degraded,
> When the thrill of them has faded
> Let's say, "Good-bye" and leave it alone.

It corresponds no less to the cockney corn of "Mad About
the Boy":

> Mad about the boy
> I know I'm potty but I'm mad about the boy.
> He sets me 'eart on fire
> With love's desire,
> In fact I've got it bad about the boy.

But wit is Coward's ultimate hedge against sentimentality. Although the duet "Something To Do with Spring"
is unabashedly rhapsodical, the lovers' emotions are cut
through with an awareness of animal nature. The result

is a lyric more lively and intelligent than is usual in such duets:

HE: The dewdrops glitter like diamond links—
SHE: Maybe it's something to do with Spring.
HE: They say that rabbits have minds like sinks—
SHE: Maybe it's something to do with Spring.
HE: The way that the sows behave
       May seem delightfully quaint.
       But why should the cows behave
       With *no* restraint?
SHE: I'd love to know what that stallion thinks—
HE: Maybe it's something to do with Spring.

Among Coward's contemporaries, only Cole Porter managed to hold romance, raciness, and wit in such sophisticated balance.

6

A Frivolous Man

In the National Portrait Gallery in London, two icons commemorate the face Noel Coward showed to the world. The first, a 1930 bust by Paul Hamann, is a smooth, bronze mask, its eyes empty and its expression blank. It captures with humor the unexpectedly bland visage that was one of Coward's public faces. In the second, a 1936 studio photograph by Norman Parkinson, the right half of Coward's face is shadowed, and a hand raised to the mouth conceals everything beneath the nose. Only a pinpoint of light reflected in the left eye relieves a total lack of expression. It is all a question of masks, Leo observes in *Design for Living*. We wear them as a form of protection for our timid souls.

The blankness of such portraiture is not discordant with the more popular icons that have come down to us — photographs of Coward drinking tea in the Nevada desert, or sprawled indecorously with Gertrude Lawrence on a sofa, or sitting in a Savonarola chair with angelic wings seeming to sprout from his shoulders. Such camp frivolity was for Coward the ultimate mask. It implied a stoical dignity that abjured the solemnity of stoicism. It was a declaration of freedom from metaphysics and morality. His best songs and plays are about frivolity, and his most lasting work has been his most insistently shallow. "Don't Let's Be Beastly to the Germans," he cooed to wartime London. "Why Must the Show Go On?" he demanded in his cabaret performance in New York. *The Vortex* is about the terrible spector of frivoli-

ty no longer possible; *Design for Living*, about frivolity
on the ropes; *Hay Fever*, *Easy Virtue*, and *Private Lives*,
about frivolity triumphant. The greatest of Coward's
plays, *Private Lives*, is the most articulate on the subject of frivolity, both its masks and its moments of honesty.

Frivolity implied mettle to Coward when it was
edged with insouciance. There is an element of fortitude
in his characters skipping away from their messes in
plays like *Design for Living*, *Blithe Spirit*, *Hay Fever*,
and *Private Lives*. Only in a superficial impression of the
plays are the characters irresponsible children. The in-
escapable ménage à trois, whether astral or earthly, is
cause for neither rebellion nor prostration in their mode
of behavior, but for a Chaplinesque pirouette. Coward
always admired such masquers. His personal writings
overflow with praise for those who "behave perfectly"
or "gaily" in difficult circumstances. "Vivien [Leigh],
with deep sadness in her heart and, for one fleeting moment, tears in her eyes, behaved gaily and charmingly
and never for one instant allowed her private unhappiness to spill over," he rhapsodized in his diary. "There
is always hope for people with that amount of courage
and consideration for others."[1]

Frivolity was even a kind of aesthetic for Coward.
Not for him the Victorian equation of amplitude and
seriousness, of facticity and probity, of solemnity and
depth. His comic plots are famous for their minimal
development and capricious denouements. What could
be more insouciant than the singing of "Même les Anges"
that concludes *Fallen Angels* or the stage laughter that
concludes *Design for Living*? His characters have little
mooring in economic realities; less, in behavioral orthodoxy; and they confront their fates with a candor not of
this world. Such mysteriously great comic lines as "This
haddock's disgusting" and "Very flat, Norfolk" are not
intellectually witty but gamesome and blithe — brilliant

throwaways that make the cleverness of Wilde seem labored. "Coward took the fat off English comic dialogue," Kenneth Tynan once observed.[2] It is equally true to say that The Master put dramaturgy itself on a diet, and that the result was comedy as elegantly and stylishly trim as he was himself.

Coward's melodramas are esteemed less than his comedies, of course, and rightly so. Many of these long-unstaged plays are comparable to the most durable works of Maugham or Lonsdale, but even the best of them play tribute to orthodoxies of conduct that the comedies pare away, disclosing trivialities that enchant us. Coward was so much the master of trivialities that in other modes and other moods he seems not quite himself, not quite "The Master."

Frivolity was ultimately style for Coward, not just *a* style, but *style* — the dashing extravagance that puts impudent fate in its place and that says, "I am what I choose to be." To style's efficacy as his professional trademark, the fabulous dressing gowns stand silent witness today in museums. To its timeless appeal as an aesthetic, his comedies stand living witness on the stage. To its winged spirit in his person, countless anecdotes and numerous tributes are memorial. Even a magazine advertisement published shortly before his death testifies to The Master's incomparable élan. As part of a series of advertisements, he was asked what things, in his view, had style. His reply was quintessentially Coward:

A candy-striped Jeep; Jane Austen; Cassius Clay; *The Times* before it changed; Danny La Rue; Charleston in South Carolina; "Monsieur" de Givenchy; a zebra (but *not* a zebra crossing); evading boredom; Gertrude Lawrence; the Paris Opera House; white; a seagull; a Brixham trawler; Margot Fonteyn; any Cole Porter song; English pageantry; Marlene's voice . . . and . . . Lingfield has a tiny bit.

Notes

1. THE LEGEND AND THE LIFE

1. David Niven, *The Moon's a Balloon* (London: Hamish Hamilton, 1971), 302.
2. The anecdote is related by Cole Lesley, *Remembered Laughter: The Life of Noel Coward* (New York: Knopf, 1977), 138. Olivier relates kindred stories about the imaginary Roger. *See* Laurence Olivier, *Confessions of an Actor: An Autobiography* (New York: Simon and Schuster, 1982), 62–63.
3. Unidentified quotation by Lesley, *Remembered Laughter*, 364. The passage does not appear in *The Noël Coward Diaries*, ed. Graham Payn and Sheridan Morley (Boston: Little, Brown, 1982).
4. *The Noël Coward Diaries*, 21 December 1967.
5. Noel Coward, *Present Indicative: An Autobiography* (New York: Doubleday, 1947), 73.
6. *The Noël Coward Diaries*, 6 August 1956.
7. Vera Brittain, *Testament of Youth* (New York: Seaview, 1980), 154.
8. Coward, *Present Indicative*, 77.
9. Dates of plays given in parentheses are those of the first professional production, British or American, stage or television.
10. George Bernard Shaw to Noel Coward, 27 June 1921. The letter is held in the Humanities Research collection at the University of Texas.
11. *Daily Graphic*, 29 November 1924.
12. *Chips: The Diaries of Sir Henry Channon*, ed. Robert Rhodes James (London: Weidenfeld and Nicholson, 1967), 8 September 1945.

13. Lesley went on to write the best Coward biography to
     date, *Remembered Laughter*. Payn collaborated with
     Sheridan Morley in editing *The Noël Coward Diaries*.
14. *Sunday Chronicle* (London), 26 April 1925.
15. William Somerset Maugham, Introduction to *Bitter Sweet
     and Other Plays* by Noel Coward (Garden City, N. Y.:
     Doubleday, Doran, 1929), v, vii.
16. Coward, *Present Indicative*, 260.
17. Kenneth Tynan, "A Tribute to Mr. Coward," *A View of
     the English Stage, 1944–63* (London: Poynter, 1975),
     137.
18. Cited in Cole Lesley, Graham Payn, and Sheridan Mor-
     ley, eds., *Noël Coward and His Friends* (New York: Mor-
     row, 1979), 132.
19. George Devine, diary entry for September 1943. Unpub-
     lished.
20. Sean O'Casey, *The Green Crow* (New York: Braziller,
     1956), 88.
21. *The Noël Coward Diaries*, 19 September 1952.
22. *The Noël Coward Diaries*, 31 December 1956.
23. In conversation. *See* Graham Payn and Sheridan Morley,
     eds., *The Noël Coward Diaries*, 59 n.
24. *The Noël Coward Diaries*, 1 July 1946.
25. Tynan, 137.
26. *The Noël Coward Diaries*, 27 September 1956.
27. *The Noël Coward Diaries*, 2 July 1962.
28. *The Noël Coward Diaries*, 2 September 1963.
29. *The Noël Coward Diaries*, 11 September 1960.
30. *Sunday Times* (London), 15, 22, and 29 January 1961.
31. *The Noël Coward Diaries*, 29 October 1961.
32. *The Noël Coward Diaries*, 5 October 1963.
33. Cited in Lesley, Foreward to *Remembered Laughter*, xx.
34. *The Noël Coward Diaries*, 12 February 1956.
35. *The Times* (London), 25 May 1973.

2. The Comedies of Manners

1. "It's no good, I simply cannot abide Restoration comedy.
    I am sure it was good in its time, but now its obvious,
    bawdy roguishness bores the hell out of me. *Love for*

Love seems to me to be appallingly overwritten. It is, I suppose, kind of critics to compare me with Congreve, but I do wish they hadn't." *The Noël Coward Diaries*, ed. Graham Payn and Sheridan Morley (Boston: Little, Brown, 1982), 22 November 1964.

2. Charles Lamb, "On the Artificial Comedies of the Last Century," *The Essays of Elia*, ed. William Macdonald (London: Dent and Sons, 1914), 283.

3. Thomas Babington Macaulay, "Comic Dramatists of the Restoration," vol. 3 of *Critical and Historical Essays*, 9th ed. (London: Longman, Brown Green, Longmans, Roberts, 1858), 157.

4. George Meredith, *An Essay on Comedy and the Uses of the Comic Spirit*, ed. Lane Cooper (New York: Scribner's, 1918), 83.

5. Noel Coward, *Present Indicative: An Autobiography* (New York: Doubleday, 1947), 179.

6. Coward, Introduction to *Play Parade*, vol. 1 (Garden City, N. Y.: Doubleday, Doran, 1933), xi.

7. Coward, Introduction to *Play Parade*, vol. 1, xi.

8. "To me, the essence of good comedy writing is that perfectly ordinary phrases such as 'Just fancy!' should, by virtue of their context, achieve greater laughs than the most literate epigrams. Some of the biggest laughs in *Hay Fever* occur on such lines as 'Go on', 'No there isn't, is there?' and 'This haddock's disgusting.'" Coward, as quoted by Cole Lesley, *Remembered Laughter: The Life of Noel Coward* (New York: Knopf, 1977), 434.

9. Coward, *Present Indicative*, 204–05.

10. Coward, *Present Indicative*, 320.

11. Coward, *Present Indicative*, 320.

12. L. J. Potts, *Comedy* (London: Hutchinson's University Library, 1948), 151.

13. Jessica Milner Davis, *Farce* (London: Methuen, 1978), 88.

14. Coward, *Present Indicative*, 122.

15. Coward, *Present Indicative*, 137.

16. Quoted in Lesley, *Remembered Laughter*, 150.

17. Brooks Atkinson, *The New York Times*, 25 January 1933.

18. *The Times* (London), 26 January 1939.

19.   Otto's speech in Act II is a classic defense of homosexuality although that is not its ostensible subject.
20.   Coward, Introduction to *Play Parade*, vol. 1, xvii.
21.   George Jean Nathan, *Passing Judgments* (Rutherford, N. J.: Fairleigh Dickinson University Press, 1970), 147–48. Sean O'Casey enlarged on Nathan's argument in "Coward Codology II" in *The Green Crow* (New York: Braziller, 1956), 97–107.
22.   *The Noël Coward Diaries*, 23 March 1951.
23.   *The Noël Coward Diaries*, 26 March 1951.

3. The Light Comedies

1.   Several academic studies have been made of such influences. *See* especially Carolyn Sherrill Rogers, "Dramatic Structure in the Comedies of Noël Coward: The Influence of the Festive Tradition," Ph.D. diss., Florida State University, 1972, and Donald Phillip Hill, "The Selected Comedies of Noël Coward: An Analysis of Comic Technique," Ph.D. diss., University of Michigan, 1977.
2.   Noel Coward, *Present Indicative: An Autobiography* (New York: Doubleday, 1947), 210.
3.   Cole Lesley, *Remembered Laughter: The Life of Noel Coward* (New York: Knopf, 1977), 87.
4.   Coward, *Future Indefinite* (Garden City, N. Y.: Doubleday, 1954), 15.
5.   *The Noël Coward Diaries*, ed. Graham Payn and Sheridan Morley (Boston: Little, Brown, 1982), 7 February 1947.
6.   Coward played Garry Essendine in the 1942 tour, in the 1942 run in London, for the first three months of the 1947 London revival, and in alternation with the role of Sebastien in *Nude with Violin* in America in 1958.
7.   *See*, for instance, Frank Rich's review of the George C. Scott production of *Present Laughter*, in which Essendine is characterized as "a debonair British lounge lizard with 'a glittering veneer.'" Rich goes on to observe, "As a play, *Present Laughter* is less about the Coward style than the Coward persona." *The New York Times*, 16 July 1982.

8. Coward was fond of inserting such passages into his plays. *See*, for instance, the famous exchange between Cuckoo and Boffin in *South Sea Bubble*, Act II, Scene I.

9. John Lahr, *Coward the Playwright* (London: Methuen, 1982), 32.

10. *Blithe Spirit* was the longest running straight play in London theater history until 1957, when Agatha Christie's *The Mousetrap* surpassed its record.

11. Coward, Introduction to *Play Parade*, vol. 5 (London: Heinemann, 1958), xxxii.

12. Lahr, 117.

13. *The Noël Coward Diaries*, 11 July 1941.

14. *See* especially Rose Snider, *Satire in the Comedies of Congreve, Sheridan, Wilde, and Coward*, University of Maine Studies, Second Series, no. 42 (Orono, Me.: University Press, 1937). Coward himself disliked the comparison. *See* chapter 2, note 1 above.

15. George Jean Nathan, *Art of the Night* (New York: Knopf, 1928), 22.

16. *The Times* (London), 8 September 1952.

17. Atkinson did not explicitly mention the French dance known as a quadrille, but one suspects he had it in mind as a source of the play's title. *The New York Times*, 4 November 1954.

18. Brooks Atkinson described Axel's rhapsody about railroading in America as "some excellent writing." *The New York Times*, 4 November 1954. Geoffrey Tarran in the *Morning Advertiser* (13 September 1952) wrote: "When he declares his belief in the value of railroads in the fostering of American unity and prosperity and describes the scenic beauties surrounding the tracks, he strikingly proves how lyrical a man can be over tasks to which he is devoted."

19. *The Noël Coward Diaries*, 17 November 1957.

20. The original script of *Nude with Violin* calls for a final tableau in which Lauderdale is seen completing "Nude with Violin" in an empty studio. The tableau was cut between the Dublin opening in September 1956 and the London opening on 7 November 1956.

21. *The New York Times*, 15 November 1957.

4. The Melodramas

1. Interviewed by *The New York Times* for his seventieth
    birthday, Coward stressed that he had no social causes
    in his plays, that he wanted only "to write good plays,
    to grip as well as amuse." *The New York Times*, 14
    November 1969.
2. Noel Coward, *Present Indicative: An Autobiography*
    (Garden City, N. Y.: Doubleday, 1947), 180.
3. Coward himself had a horror of drugs and, according to
    Cole Lesley, sampled marijuana only once. The exper-
    iment convinced him momentarily that he was dying and
    was never repeated. *See* Cole Lesley, *Remembered
    Laughter: The Life of Noel Coward* (New York: Knopf,
    1977), 46.
4. *Sunday Times* (London), 30 November 1924.
5. The emotional thralldom in which his own mother held
    Coward all his life must have had something to do with
    this concern for tots, but neither Viola Coward nor any-
    one else has ever seen her portrait in the mothers Coward
    lampooned—certainly not in Mrs. Worthington, the
    eponymous stagemother he celebrated in song and who
    might be assumed to resemble Mrs. Coward.
6. *The New York Times*, 8 December 1925.
7. *Sunday Times* (London), 13 June 1926.
8. "The line that was intended to establish the play on a
    basis of comedy rather than tragedy comes at the end of
    the second act when Larita, the heroine, irritated beyond
    endurance by the smug attitude of her 'in-laws,' argues
    them out of the room and collapses on to the sofa where,
    suddenly catching sight of a statuette of the Venus de
    Milo on a pedestal, she shies a book at it and says: 'I
    always hated that damned thing!'" Coward, *Present In-
    dicative*, 229.
9. "The narrow-mindedness, the moral righteousness and
    the over-rigid social codes have disappeared but with
    them has gone much that was graceful, well-behaved,
    and endearing. It was in a mood of nostalgic regret at
    the decline of such conventions that I wrote *Easy Virtue*."
    Coward, Introduction to *Play Parade*, vol. 2 (London:
    Heinemann, 1950), ix.

10. *Sunday Times* (London), 13 June 1926.

11. Coward, *Present Indicative*, 334–35.

12. In the first academic study of Coward's writing, Meyer Levin called the play "a collection of once fashionable attitudes only sporadically relieved by the sound of a living voice." *Noel Coward* (New York: Twayne, 1968), 142. The critic John Lahr has more recently referred to *Post Mortem* as "a flabby jab at the futility of war." *Coward the Playwright* (London: Methuen, 1982), 94.

13. *The Noël Coward Diaries*, ed. Graham Payn and Sheridan Morley (Boston: Little, Brown, 1982), 12 February 1956.

14. Lesley, *Remembered Laughter*, 249.

15. *The Noël Coward Diaries*, 3 November 1946.

16. Coward, Introduction to *Play Parade*, vol. 5 (London: Heinemann, 1958), xxvi–xxvii.

17. Coward, *Present Indicative*, 349.

18. The play was in fact designed for a revolving stage at the Coliseum, but the stage was not available and Coward had to be content with six hydraulic lifts at the Theatre Royal. C. B. Cochran, the producer, is alleged to have counted forty-five such misstatements in the press. *See* Cole Lesley, Graham Payn, and Sheridan Morley, *Noël Coward and His Friends* (New York: Morrow, 1979), 87–88.

19. Coward, *Present Indicative*, 351. Alan Parsons in the *Daily Mail* (1 November 1931) reported a slightly different version of the remark: "After all, it is a pretty exciting thing in these days to be English."

20. Coward, *Present Indicative*, 352.

21. *Daily Mail*, 1 November 1931.

22. So speculated *The Post*, 14 October 1931.

23. *See* A. J. P. Taylor, *English History: 1914–1945* (New York: Oxford, 1965), 314.

24. Ethel Mannin, "A Play Which Makes Me Rage," *The New Leader*, 29 January 1932.

25. Coward, *Present Indicative*, 352.

26. Lahr, 103.

27. Coward, *Present Indicative*, 352.

28. Coward, Introduction to *Play Parade*, vol. 4 (London: Heinemann, 1954), xiv.

29.   *See* Lesley, *Remembered Laughter*, 204.
30.   *Daily Telegraph*, 1 May 1943.
31.   Ward Morehouse, "'Dear Noel' on Love and Marriage," *Theatre Arts* 40 (November 1956): 18.
32.   Douglas Dunn, "Pity the Poor Philosophers: Coward's Comic Genius," *Encounter* (October 1980): 51.
33.   *The Noël Coward Diaries*, 1 May 1958.
34.   *The Noël Coward Diaries*, 22 April 1960.
35.   *Daily Mail*, 9 September 1960.
36.   *Sunday Times* (London), 15, 22, and 29 January 1961.
37.   Coward had dealt with many aging actresses — Edith Evans among the most notable. In a production of *Hay Fever* she persisted in saying, "On a very clear day you can see Marlow," incorrectly interpolating the "very." Finally Coward instructed her, "Edith, on a clear day you can see Marlow. On a *very* clear day you can see Marlow *and* Beaumont *and* Fletcher."
38.   *The Noël Coward Diaries*, 28 August 1962.
39.   Upon attending a performance of Neil Simon's *Plaza Suite*, Coward wrote in his diaries, "Such a good idea having different plays all played in a hotel suite! I wonder where Neil Simon got it from?" *The Noël Coward Diaries*, 6 April 1969.
40.   *Daily Mail*, April 15, 1966.
41.   *Come into the Garden Maud* and a shortened version of *A Song at Twilight* were produced in New York in 1974 under the title *Noël Coward in Two Keys*. The production script was prepared by Charles Kindl.
42.   *The Noël Coward Diaries*, 17 July 1965.
43.   David Cecil, *Max: A Biography* (London: Constable, 1964).

5. The Revues, Operettas, and Songs

1.   *Morning Post*, 1 May 1925.
2.   "World Weary" was written for the New York production of the revue and was not heard in the London production.
3.   *Observer*, 25 March 1928.

4. Noel Coward, *Future Indefinite: An Autobiography* (New York: Doubleday, 1954), 330.

5. *The Times* (London), 23 August 1945.

6. "Uncle Harry" was in the original score of *Pacific 1860* but was removed before production. Although later replaced, it does not appear in the quasi-official *Play Parade* version of *Pacific 1860*.

7. Coward, Introduction to *The Lyrics of Noël Coward* (Woodstock, N.Y.: Overlook, 1973), vii.

8. Coward published a selection of his poetry in *Not Yet the Dodo and Other Verses* (Garden City, N.Y.: Doubleday, 1968).

9. Quoted in Cole Lesley, *Remembered Laughter: The Life of Noel Coward* (New York: Knopf, 1977), 208.

10. A number of Coward's songs exist in several versions, particularly those he adapted for American performance. Versions quoted in this chapter are all from *The Lyrics of Noël Coward*.

6. A FRIVOLOUS MAN

1. *The Noël Coward Diaries*, ed. Graham Payn and Sheridan Morley (Boston: Little, Brown, 1982), 1 January 1960.

2. Kenneth Tynan, "In Memory of Mr. Coward," *The Sound of Two Hands Clapping* (London: Cape, 1975), 60.

Bibliography

Works by Noel Coward

A. Autobiography

Present Indicative: An Autobiography. London: Heinemann; New York: Doubleday, Doran, 1937.

Australia Visited. London: Heinemann, 1941.

Middle East Diary. London: Heinemann; New York: Doubleday, Doran, 1944.

Future Indefinite: An Autobiography. London: Heinemann; New York: Doubleday, Doran, 1954.

The Noël Coward Diaries, ed. Graham Payn and Sheridan Morley. Boston: Little, Brown, 1982.

B. Collected Plays

Collected Sketches and Lyrics. London: Hutchinson, 1931; New York: Doubleday, Doran, 1932.

Play Parade. 6 vols. London: Heinemann, 1934–62.

Volume 1 (1934): *Design for Living, Cavalcade, Private Lives, Bitter Sweet, Post-Mortem, The Vortex, Hay Fever*.

Volume 2 (1939): *This Year of Grace!, Words and Music, Operette, Conversation Piece, Fallen Angels, Easy Virtue*.

Volume 3 (1950): *The Queen Was in the Parlour, "I'll Leave It to You," The Young Idea, Sirocco, The Rat Trap, "This Was a Man," Home Chat, The Marquise*.

Volume 4 (1954): *Tonight at 8:30 [We Were Dancing, The Astonished Heart, "Red Peppers," Hands Across the Sea, Fumed Oak, Shadow Play, Ways and Means,*

Still Life, Family Album], *Present Laughter, This Happy Breed.*

Volume 5 (1958): *Pacific 1860, "Peace in Our Time," Relative Values, Quadrille, Blithe Spirit.*

Volume 6 (1962): *Point Valaine, South Sea Bubble, Ace of Clubs, Nude with Violin, Waiting in the Wings.*

Coward Plays. 5 vols. Introductions by Raymond Mander and Joe Mitchenson. The Master Playwrights Series. London: Methuen, 1979–83.

Volume 1 (1979): *Hay Fever, The Vortex, Fallen Angels, Easy Virtue.*

Volume 2 (1979): *Private Lives, Bitter Sweet, The Marquise, Post-Mortem.*

Volume 3 (1979): *Design for Living, Cavalcade, Conversation Piece, Tonight at 8:30 (1) [Hands Across the Sea, Still Life, Fumed Oak].*

Volume 4 (1979): *Blithe Spirit, Present Laughter, This Happy Breed, Tonight at 8:30 (2) [Ways and Means, The Astonished Heart, "Red Peppers"].*

Volume 5 (1983): *Relative Values, Look After Lulu!, Waiting in the Wings, Suite in Three Keys [A Song at Twilight, Shadows of the Evening, Come into the Garden Maud].*

C. NOVEL

Pomp and Circumstance. London: Heinemann; New York: Doubleday, 1960.

D. SATIRES

A Withered Nosegay. London: Christophers, 1922. Published, with additions, in the United States as *Terribly Intimate Portraits*, New York: Boni and Liveright, 1922.

Chelsea Buns. London: Hutchinson, 1925.

Spangled Unicorn. London: Hutchinson, 1932; New York: Frisch, 1982.

E. SHORT STORY COLLECTIONS

To Step Aside. London: Heinemann; New York: Doubleday, Doran, 1939.

Star Quality. London: Heinemann; New York: Doubleday, Doran, 1951.

Pretty Polly Barlow and Other Stories. London: Heinemann, 1964; New York: Doubleday, 1965.

Bon Voyage. London: Heinemann, 1967; New York: Doubleday, 1968.

The Collected Stories of Noël Coward. New York: Dutton, 1983.

F. VERSE COLLECTIONS

The Noël Coward Song Book. London: Michael Joseph, 1953; New York: Methuen, 1984.

The Lyrics of Noël Coward. London: Heinemann, 1965; New York: Doubleday, 1967; Woodstock, N.Y.: Overlook, 1973.

Not Yet the Dodo. London: Heinemann, 1967; New York: Doubleday, 1968.

The Collected Verse of Noel Coward, ed. Graham Payn and Martin Tickner. New York: Methuen, 1985.

WORKS ABOUT NOEL COWARD

A. BOOKS

Braybrooke, Patrick. *The Amazing Mr. Noël Coward*. London: Archer, 1933.

Castle, Charles. *Noël*. London: Allen, 1972.

Greacen, Robert. *The Art of Noël Coward*. Aldington, England: Hand and Flower, 1953.

Lahr, John. *Coward the Playwright*. London: Methuen, 1982.

Lesley, Cole. *The Life of Noel Coward*. London: Cape, 1976. Published in the United States as *Remembered Laughter: The Life of Noel Coward*, New York: Knopf, 1976.

————, Graham Payn, and Sheridan Morley, eds. *Noël Coward and His Friends*. London: Weidenfeld and Nicholson; New York: Doubleday, 1979.

Levin, Milton. *Noël Coward*. New York: Twayne, 1968.

Mander, Raymond, and Joe Mitchenson. *Theatrical Companion to Coward*. London: Rockliff; New York: Macmillan, 1957.

Morley, Sheridan. *A Talent to Amuse*. London: Heinemann; New York: Doubleday, 1969; Boston: Little, Brown, 1985.

B. ARTICLES, PARTS OF BOOKS, DISSERTATIONS, AND THESES

Agate, James, "The Ingenium of Noël Coward." In *My Theatre Talks*, pp. 185–92. New York: Blom, 1971.

Albee, Edward. "Notes for Noël About Coward." Introduction to *Three Plays by Noël Coward*, pp. 3–6. New York: Grove, 1965.

Bennett, Arnold. Introduction to *The Plays of Noël Coward*, pp. v–xi. Garden City, N.Y.: Doubleday, Doran, 1928.

Bryden, Ronald. "Halfway House" [*Hay Fever*]. In *The Unfinished Hero and Other Essays*, pp. 51–56. London: Faber and Faber, 1969.

Catsiapis, Helene. "Noël Coward et la France." *Revue d'histoire du theatre* 33 (1981): 83–96.

Clem, Judith Jean. "A Study of Five Comic Techniques in Three Plays by Noël Coward." Master's thesis, California State University, 1973.

Comden, Betty, and Adolph Green. "Noël Coward." In *Double Exposure*, ed. Roddy McDowall, pp. 33–35. New York: Delacorte, 1966.

De Kuyper, Eric. "Dear Noël." *Kunst en Cultuur* (19 April 1973): 14.

Dunn, Douglas. "Pity the Poor Philosopher: Coward's Comic Genius." *Encounter* (October 1980): 49–51.

Ervine, St. John. "The Plays of Mr. Noël Coward." *Queen's Quarterly* 43 (Spring 1935), 1–21.

Hill, Donald Phillip. "The Selected Comedies of Noël Coward: An Analysis of Comic Techniques." Ph.D. diss., University of Minnesota, 1977.

Lahr, John. "Noël Coward." In *Automatic Vaudeville: Essays on Star Turns*, pp. 22–40. New York: Knopf, 1984.

Maugham, Somerset. Introduction to *Bitter Sweet and Other Plays* by Noël Coward, pp. v–xiii. Garden City, N.Y.: Doubleday, Doran, 1929.

Morehouse, Ward. "'Dear Noël' on Love and Marriage." *Theatre Arts* 40 (November 1956): 17–19, 84.

Morse, Clarence R. "Mad Dogs and Englishmen: A Study of Noël Coward." *Emporia State Research Studies* 21 (1973): 5–50.

Nathan, George Jean. "Mr. Coward" [*Design for Living*]. In *Passing Judgments*, pp. 147–58. Rutherford, N.J.: Fairleigh Dickinson University Press, 1970.

_____. "Noël Coward" [*Point Valaine*]. In *The Theatre of the Moment: A Journalistic Commentary*, pp. 279–82. New York: Knopf, 1936.

O'Casey, Sean. "Coward Codology." In *The Green Crow*, pp. 87–115. New York: Braziller, 1956.

Otten, Terry. "'Played to the Finish': Coward and Albee." *Studies in the Humanities* 6 (1977): 31–36.

Real, Jere. "The Playwright as Bohemian Tory." *Intercollegiate Review* II (1975): 95–101.

Rogers, Carolyn Sherrill White. "Dramatic Structure in the Comedies of Noël Coward: The Influence of the Festive Tradition." Ph.D. diss., Florida State University, 1972.

Rubin, Donna Sue. "Sir Noël Coward: Director." Master's thesis. Adelphi University, 1977.

Snider, Rose. "Noël Coward." In *Satire in the Comedies of Congreve, Sheridan, Wilde, and Coward*, pp. 95–123. University of Maine Studies, second series, no. 42. Oron, Me.: University Press, 1937.

Trewin, J. C. "Tap-Tap: Noël Coward." In *Dramatists of Today*, pp. 151–61. London: Staples, 1953.

Tynan, Kenneth. "A Tribute to Mr. Coward." In *A View of the English Stage, 1944–63*, pp. 135–37. London: Poynter, 1975.

_____. "In Memory of Mr. Coward." In *The Sound of Two Hands Clapping*, pp. 58–63. London: Cape, 1975.

Whiting, John. "Coward Cruising." In *John Whiting on Theatre*, pp. 101–08. London: Ross, 1966.

Index